P9-DFK-969

SSF

The Smithsonian National Air and Space Museum

Book of Flight

Judith E. Rinard

FIREFLY BOOKS

A FIREFLY BOOK

SHUTTLE LIFTOFF

Cover: Blasting into the sky, the space shuttle *Endeavour* roars toward space.

AMAZING SIGHT

Page1: British children watch as the monoplane of Louis Blériot soars above the English coast. This photograph was probably taken soon after Blériot's historic flight across the English Channel in 1909.

IN PERFECT FORM

Pages 2-3: Flying in close formation, the U.S. Air Force Thunderbirds practice a high-speed maneuver.

SPACE REPAIR

Page 5: During a 1973 spacewalk, astronaut Owen Garriott deploys a solar shield to shade the U.S. space station Skylab from the Sun.

Published by Firefly Books Ltd. 2007

Copyright © 2007 Judith E. Rinard

All rights reserved. No part of this publication may be reproduced, stored in a retrieval system, or transmitted in any form or by any means, electronic, mechanical, photocopying, recording or otherwise, without the prior written permission of the Publisher.

First printing

Publisher Cataloging-in-Publication Data (U.S.)
Rinard, Judith E.
    Book of flight : Smithsonian National Air and Space Museum / Judith E. Rinard.
2nd rev. and updated ed.
[128] p. : col. photos. ; cm.
Includes index.
Summary: The major milestones in flight history illustrated from the collections of the National Air and Space Museum. Includes the development of flight and diagrams explaining flight science and technology.
ISBN-13: 978-1-55407-292-7
ISBN-10: 1-55407-292-1
ISBN-13: 978-1-55407-275-0 (pbk.)
ISRN-10: 1-55407-275-1 (pbk.)
1. Aeronautics — History. 2. Aeronautics — United States — History. 3. National Air and Space Museum. I. Title.
629.13/ 009 dc22   TL515.R55 2007

Library and Archives Canada Cataloguing in Publication
Rinard, Judith E
    Book of flight : the Smithsonian National Air and Space Museum / Judith
E. Rinard. — 2nd ed., rev. and updated
Includes index.
ISBN-13: 978-1-55407-292-7 (bound)
ISBN-13: 978-1-55407-275-0 (pbk.)
ISBN-10: 1-55407-292-1 (bound)
ISBN-10: 1-55407-275-1 (pbk.)
1. National Air and Space Museum. 2. Aeronautics—United States—History.
3. Astronautics—United States—History. 4. Aeronautics—History. I. National Air and Space Museum II. Title.
TL506.U62W37 2007   629.1074'753   C2007-900277-3

Published in the United States by
Firefly Books (U.S.) Inc.
P.O. Box 1338, Ellicott Station
Buffalo, New York 14205

Published in Canada by
Firefly Books Ltd.
66 Leek Crescent
Richmond Hill, Ontario L4B 1H1

Produced by
Charles O. Hyman, Visual Communications, Inc., Washington, D.C.

Designed by
Kevin R. Osborn, Research & Design, Ltd., Arlington, Virginia

Smithsonian Institution
Publication Director   Patricia Graboske
Manager Educational Programs   Clare Cuddy
Chief Photo Archivist   Melissa A. N. Keiser
Photography by   Mark Avino, Eric F. Long, Carolyn Russo

Printed in China

The publisher gratefully acknowledges the financial support for our publishing program by the Government of Canada through the Book Publishing Industry Development Program.

ACKNOWLEDGEMENTS

The author gratefully acknowledges the assistance of the curators and other staff at the National Air and Space Museum who made this book possible. Dominick Pisano, Chairman of the Aeronautics Division, and Michael Neufeld, Curator in the Space History Division, read the manuscript and offered many helpful suggestions. Valerie Neal, Curator in Space History, gave assistance and answered questions throughout the project. Special thanks to Melissa Keiser of the Archives Division, who gathered the photographs for the book and patiently answered questions about them with detailed and highly useful information. Thanks also to Clare Cuddy, Manager of Educational Programs, and Patricia Graboske, Chief of Publications, for their invaluable assistance throughout the project.

The photo editor gratefully acknowledges the assistance of her colleagues at the National Air and Space Museum, particularly Dana Bell, Kate Igoe, Kristine Kaske, Dan Hagedorn, and Brian Nicklas (Archives) for historical and photographic assistance; Barbara Weitbrecht (Archives) for unflagging IT support; Joanne London (Aeronautics) for assistance with the Poster Collection; Alex Spencer (Aeronautics) for assistance with the trophy and flight materiel collections as well as assistance in scanning images; David Gant (Exhibits) for assistance in scanning images; Cathleen Lewis and Martin Collins (Space History) for assistance with Soviet photographs and artifacts; Rose Steinat, Priscilla Strain and Andrew Johnston (Center for Earth and Planetary Studies) for assistance with photography and maps; and the NASM Office of Information Technology for IT support.

Supplementary information for this 2007 edition was provided by Thomas B. Allen and Roger MacBride Allen.

Contents

Introduction

IMAGE a time when people only dreamed of flying, when the sight of a jet streaking across the sky would have been astounding, and the idea of launching a rocket into space too fantastic to comprehend. You may be surprised to learn that time was not very long ago. It is possible that someone you know was born before airliners and jets even existed.

The stories you are about to read—and the amazing pictures you will see—capture the wonder and excitement of a history that is still unfolding. At the dawn of the 20th century, the first powered aircraft took to the skies. Now the International Space Station is a reality. And in the first years of the new millennium, engineers are developing reusable space vehicles, designing airplanes that will fly at five times the speed of sound, and exploring a human mission to Mars.

The pioneers of flight paved the way for a future filled with adventure and achievement, a fact demonstrated every day at the Smithsonian National Air and Space Museum's two sites—the flagship building on the National Mall in Washington and the Steven F. Udvar-Hazy Center in Chantilly, Virginia.

Filled with history-making aircraft and spacecraft, our buildings bring to life the work of the inventors and scientists who created these machines, and explain how our world is changing because of the progress in aviation and space exploration. *The Smithsonian National Air and Space Museum Book of Flight* celebrates the museum's famous collection and reveals highlights of its many exhibitions and displays.

In this book, for example, you will be introduced to Wilbur and Orville Wright. As children, they made and flew kites. When they got older, they designed and built bicycles. Soon they were able to put their mechanical skills to use in achieving their dream and on December 17, 1903, on a wind-swept beach near Kitty Hawk, North Carolina, they flew their first powered airplane. Millions of people come to see the original Wright

Flyer at the Mall building every year. In this book, you'll also meet Samuel Pierpont Langley, a scientist and engineer who ran the Smithsonian Institution and competed with the Wrights to build the first piloted powered flying machine. His failed *Great Aerodrome* hangs in the Udvar-Hazy Center.

People also come to the Mall building to see other early airplanes like the *Spirit of St. Louis*. In it, a 25-year-old airmail pilot named Charles Lindbergh flew nonstop from New York to Paris in 1927, a 33½-hour flight. Five years later, Amelia Earhart became the first woman pilot to fly solo across the Atlantic. Her bright red Lockheed Vega sits in the Mall. At the Udvar-Hazy Center, you'll see another Vega, Wiley Post's *Winnie Mae*, which made two record-setting around-the-world flights in the early 1930s.

Aviation's powerful influence on world history is shown in military exhibits. In the *Book of Flight*, you'll learn all about famous battles and discover how the first bombers and fighter planes worked. You will meet heroes like America's World War I flying ace, Captain Eddie Rickenbacker, as well as other military legends such as Baron Manfred von Richthofen, also known as the "Red Baron."

The courage of World War II fliers is shown in the inspiring story of the Tuskegee Airmen, the first African-American fighter pilots. This skilled and daring group fought against great odds to defend our country on two fronts—against the enemy in Europe and against racial prejudice at home.

Both the Mall building and the Udvar-Hazy Center feature famed artifacts from the major wars of the 20th century. The museum continues to collect the

Touch the Moon

A young visitor at the National Air and Space Museum delights in touching the Moonrock, collected by Apollo 17 astronauts in 1972. The Museum is one of only two places on Earth where visitors can touch lunar rock. The other is Johnson Space Center in Houston, Texas.

Hands-on Learning

In the Hall of Air Transportation, interpreter Katherine Tuow helps young visitors compare early passenger aviation with modern travel. She shows them a model DC-3 airliner and lets them try on early and recent pilot uniforms from a "Discovery Cart."

▽ Indoor Air Show

Historic aircraft surround and hover over visitors to the Boeing Aviation Hangar at the Steven F. Udvar-Hazy Center. Suspended aircraft hang at angles showing typical flight maneuvers. Lofty walkways provide close-up views of suspended aircraft.

▷ Reaching for the Sky

The Steven F. Udvar-Hazy Center, named after its leading donor, is topped by a tower that gives visitors views of flights at nearby Dulles International Airport. The center is a companion to the Air and Space Museum on the National Mall in Washington.

newest fighter aircraft, including those that are controlled by crews who remain on the ground.

By the middle of the 20th century, aircraft designers were focusing on speed. Suspended from the Mall building's ceiling is the Bell *X-1*, a bright orange, bullet-shaped plane equipped with a rocket engine. In 1947, test pilot Chuck Yeager accelerated Bell *X-1* to 700 miles per hour to break the sound barrier for the first time. At the Udvar-Hazy Center, you'll see a real Concorde, the only successful airliner to carry passengers beyond the speed of sound.

Not long after supersonic flight was achieved, the race to conquer space was on. In 1962, America's effort to orbit the Earth was successful. Astronaut John Glenn's Mercury *Friendship 7* capsule is in a Mall gallery. At both Air and Space sites, hundreds of displays and artifacts—rockets, capsules, tools, vehicles, equipment, space suits, even space food—tell the remarkable story of space exploration. In the Udvar-Hazy Center you can even see the special quarantine trailer that was home to the first moonwalkers after they returned to Earth. They were kept inside the trailer in case they had brought back moon "germs." Thankfully they didn't. One of the Mall building's most popular displays features a rock taken from the lunar surface in 1972 by Apollo astronauts.

The Air and Space Museum, on the National Mall in Washington, D.C., is the length of three city blocks, opened in 1976 and became the world's most visited museum. The Udvar-Hazy Center, which opened in 2003 to mark the centennial of the Wright brothers' historic breakthrough, features an aviation hanger ten stories high and three football fields long.

At the Udvar-Hazy Center, many engines, rockets, satellites, helicopters, airliners, and experimental flying machines are displayed for the first time in a museum setting. The center will ultimately be home to some 200 aircraft and 200 large space artifacts.

As Director of the National Air and Space Museum, I feel I am one of the luckiest people on the planet. I have the chance to be in some of the world's most fascinating buildings every day. I also know what it is like to be in a cockpit, having served many years as a U.S. Marine Corps pilot. In addition, I played a role in the space program by working at the National Aeronautics and Space Administration. Although my career has included many roles, the one I care most about is being a father and grandfather. It is for this reason that I want to preserve and share the magnificent history and technology of aviation and space exploration.

In little over 100 years, we have come a long way. But for future generations, the best is yet to come.

General John R. "Jack" Dailey, USMC (Ret.),
Director, National Air and Space Museum

The Beginnings of Flight

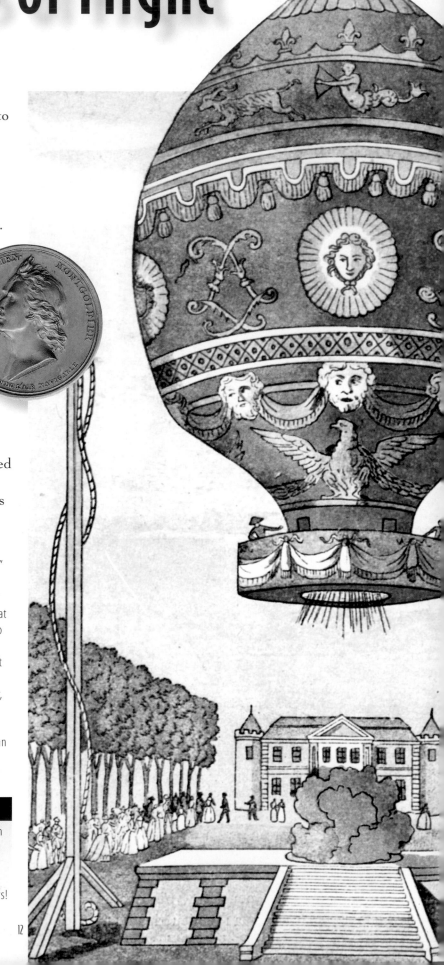

SINCE ancient times, people have dreamed of flying like birds. In Greek myths, heroes made wings to fly. In Persian legends, people zoomed through the sky on magic carpets. The ancient Chinese invented kites, and some reportedly carried humans aloft. During the Middle Ages, many people tried to fly. Some strapped on wings of cloth or feathers and jumped off towers or cliffs. Yet nothing worked, and many died.

Then in 1783, two French brothers, Joseph and Etienne Montgolfier, invented the hot-air balloon. Working in their family's paper factory, they noticed that paper put on a fire was lifted up the chimney. They filled a large cloth-and-paper bag with hot air from a fire. The hot air made the balloon lighter than air, and it rose over Paris, carrying two noblemen. This was the first recorded human flight.

In 1804, Englishman George Cayley invented the first heavier-than-air craft, a model glider. Later piloted by German Otto Lilienthal, gliders were the ancestors of the modern airplane.

◄ SIR GEORGE CAYLEY (1773-1857)

Often called the "Father of Aeronautics," Sir George Cayley first established the scientific principles of heavier-than-air flight. Studying birds, he understood that wings create a force called "lift." He also understood propulsion and control in flight and he predicted powered aircraft in the future. He first built a five-foot-long model glider based on a kite. Later, in 1853, he built a large glider that carried his unwilling coachman a short way. Afterward, the frightened coachman resigned, saying "I was hired to drive, not fly!"

FUN FACT: WHAT A GAS!

The Montgolfier brothers thought by burning straw and wool, they had created a new gas that sent their balloons into the air. They called it "Montgolfier gas." Actually, it was simply hot air. Later in 1783, Jacques Charles created the hydrogen balloon. He filled balloons with the gas hydrogen. It weighs one-fourteenth as much as air.

FUN FACT: EARLY FLIGHT PLANS

As long ago as the 15th century, Italian artist Leonardo da Vinci was designing ideas for flying machines. He sketched flapping-wing machines, called ornithopters, and even early helicopters!

Up, Up, and Away
On November 21, 1783, Jean François Pilâtre de Rozier and the Marquis d' Arlandes took off in a Montgolfier balloon before astonished Parisians. The brightly colored balloon rose 300 feet and floated for about 5 miles over Paris.

Flight Control
Lilienthal steers his glider by swinging his legs and shifting his weight. This method of control was limited and dangerous.

Gliding Pioneer
Jumping into the wind, Otto Lilienthal sails through the air in a hang glider as spectators watch. Lilienthal tested many of his glider designs by leaping off a custom-made, cone-shaped hill near Berlin. He flew over 2,500 flights, up to 64 feet high and nearly a quarter mile long.

Otto Lilienthal (1849–1896)
Otto Lilienthal was a German engineer who studied bird flight and was the first person to actively pilot, or control, a glider. Between 1891 and 1896, he built and flew 18 glider designs of lightweight cotton, willow, and bamboo. Unpowered, they glided on winds and updrafts, the same way birds soar. Lilienthal scientifically recorded his research, which greatly helped later inventors. A fearless flier, he finally crashed when he lost control in a gust of wind. He died the next day. His last words were: "Sacrifices must be made."

Go Fly a Kite
Some 19th-century thinkers returned to the idea of kites as ways to carry people aloft. Here, Alexander Graham Bell, inventor of the telephone, explains his idea for a large kite made up of many triangular surfaces.

High-Flying Act
Ballooning and gliding became exciting spectator sports in the 1800s. This 19th-century German poster features a young woman balloonist and aerial acrobat named K. Paulus.

Powered Flight: First Attempts

BALLOONING was popular in the 1800s. And with gliders, people could actually soar on wings like birds. Yet balloons and gliders were hard to control. They drifted with the wind. Inventors now began trying to achieve powered, controlled flight.

In 1852, Frenchman Henri Giffard attached a steam engine to a cigar-shaped, hydrogen-filled balloon. He called it a "dirigible," meaning steerable. Yet the airship's steam engine was heavy and the craft proved slow and still hard to maneuver. Others tried adding power to heavier-than-air flying machines. Many were bizarre contraptions. A few hovered or hopped briefly off the ground, but never flew.

In 1896, an American scientist, Dr. Samuel Langley, launched an unpiloted steam-powered model aircraft. It flew nearly a mile. Yet when Langley tried launching a large piloted version, it crashed on takeoff—twice. This seemed to prove what most people believed: powered, pilot-controlled flight was simply impossible.

▶ SAMUEL PIERPONT LANGLEY (1834-1906)

Professor Samuel P. Langley, the third secretary of the Smithsonian Institution in Washington, D.C., was a respected astronomer. The public was stunned when his unmanned steam-powered model Aerodrome No. 5 flew over the Potomac River in 1896.

In 1903, Langley attempted to launch a full-size "Great Aerodrome" with a pilot aboard. The craft was equipped with a large new gasoline engine, but no real means of control. On two attempts at takeoff, the big Aerodrome's flimsy wings collapsed. The craft sank in the water "like a handful of mortar," a newspaper reported, dumping the unlucky pilot in the river.

▶ READY FOR TAKEOFF

Men prepare the Aerodrome No. 5 for launch from a houseboat on the Potomac River. A catapult drove the steam-powered model into the air. It flew 3,300 feet before running out of steam.

FUN FACT: LEVIATHAN

Some early flying machines were huge. One, called "Leviathan," was a triple-winged monster with two steam engines and a wingspan of 103 feet! It hovered a few inches off the ground.

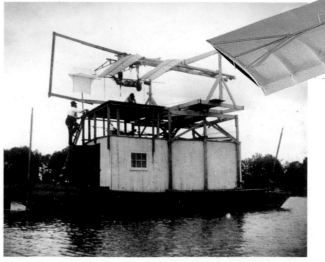

▼ Airborne!

In this painting, the launching crew watch as Aerodrome No. 5 takes flight over the Potomac in May of 1896. This unpiloted model was the first powered craft of considerable weight to fly.

D'Equevilley's Aeroplane

▲ Wings on Wheels

Inspired by the Ferris Wheel, this early French flying machine was designed by the Marquis d'Equevilley. Its multiple wings were intended to increase lift. Instead, the machine proved too heavy to lift off.

◄ Early Triplane

A different attempt at multiple-wing design was this early French triplane. Although it looked more like an airplane, the craft could not fly either.

◄ Givaudan No. 1

A third French invention, the aeroplane Givaudan No. 1 was a fanciful flying machine. Equipped with odd front and rear cyclinder wing sections, it never got off the ground.

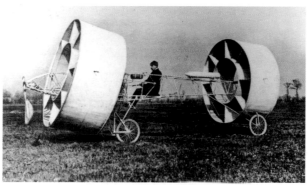

FUN FACT: ENGINE POWER

The first powered flying machines used steam engines. Yet these were much too heavy and too weak to be practical for flying large aircraft. In the late 1800s, Otto Daimler invented the first gasoline engine. Eventually, lighter-weight and more efficient gas engines helped make manned powered flight possible.

◄ Aerodrome No. 5

This model of Langley's Aerodrome No. 5 shows the machine's tandem cloth wings, twin pusher propellers, and steam engine, in center. The No. 5 had a wingspan of about 13 feet, a fourth as big as the full-size Great Aerodrome.

The Wright Brothers

O RVILLE and Wilbur Wright were fascinated by flying. As children, they received a toy rubber-band helicopter from their father. They soon copied it. As boys, they loved building and flying kites. When they grew up, they designed and built bicycles in their own business. They were brilliant mechanics.

Otto Lilienthal's work prompted the brothers to probe the puzzle of powered flight. First, they studied Cayley, Lilienthal, and others. Then they experimented and built a large glider of spruce and cotton cloth, with curved wings for lift. Next, they invented a way to control the craft's side-to-side rolling motion in the air by twisting, or warping, the wings. Last, they built a small 12-horsepower gasoline engine and attached it with bicycle chains to propellers. The result was the *Flyer*, the first powered airplane! On December 17, 1903, the brothers flew the *Flyer* at Kitty Hawk beach, North Carolina. They had at last unlocked the secret of powered, controlled human flight.

▲ BIRDWATCHING
Observing buzzards gave Wilbur his wing-warping idea. "My observations of...buzzards," he wrote, "leads me to believe that they regain their lateral balance, when partly overturned by a gust of wind, by a torsion of the tips of the wings."

► THE FIRST FLIGHT
On December 17, 1903 at Kitty Hawk, North Carolina, Orville takes off in the *Flyer*, as Wilbur watches. The flight lasted 12 seconds and covered 120 feet. A beach lifeguard took this famous photograph.

► PILOT CONTROL
A model shows how Orville controlled the *Flyer*, today in the National Air and Space Museum. He moved his hips to control wing-warping cables and moved a lever with his hand to make the *Flyer*'s nose go up or down.

FUN FACT: COIN TOSS
The brothers flipped a coin to see who would test-pilot the *Flyer* first. Wilbur won, but the *Flyer* stalled. Orville tried next, and the rest is history.

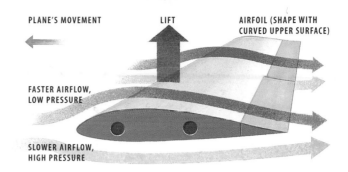

PLANE'S MOVEMENT   LIFT   AIRFOIL (SHAPE WITH CURVED UPPER SURFACE)

FASTER AIRFLOW, LOW PRESSURE

SLOWER AIRFLOW, HIGH PRESSURE

▲ How Wings Lift

An airplane's wing produces lift by its curved shape, called an "airfoil." Air passing over the rounded upper surface rushes faster than air moving over the flat bottom surface. This creates a low pressure area over the wing. The high pressure area under the wing pushes the wing upward.

▲ Pedal Power

The Wrights attached model wings to a bicycle wheel, and turned it by pedaling to test the wings' lift. The bicycle men believed a pilot could learn to control an aircraft much as a cyclist learns to balance and control a bike.

FUN FACT: THE WRIGHT STUFF

The key methods the Wrights used to achieve powered flight were: 1) wings to lift the plane; 2) an engine to propel the plane forward; and 3) movable surfaces, such as wing edges, for control. These are the same principles used to fly a Boeing 747 today.

◄ Time It!

Wilbur and Orville used this stop watch to time their historic flights at Kitty Hawk. On December 17, 1903, the *Flyer* made four flights, the longest 852 feet in 59 seconds.

◄ New Propeller

The Wrights were the first to realize an airplane propeller is really a small, twisted wing that rotates. They designed propellers of carved wood.

Wright Brothers in France

FOR years after their first flight, the Wright brothers received almost no credit or recognition for their accomplishment. Many at home and abroad scoffed and refused to believe they had even actually flown. Then in 1908, Wilbur went to France and demonstrated an improved *Flyer*, the Type A. Before a large, skeptical crowd, Wilbur took off. Soaring triumphantly into the sky, he circled the air field, making tight, steeply banked turns and perfect figure eights. The crowd went wild. Before this, they had only seen flying machines that could barely lurch off the ground and fly with little control. Wilbur was a hero. He flew over 100 demonstrations, lasting up to two hours, and took many passengers up for rides.

After these European demonstrations, the Wrights were widely accepted as masters of flight. The next year, Wright planes led the way at the world's first air meet, the 1909 Grande Semaine d'Aviation in Reims, France.

▼ FRENCH SOUVENIR

Back in America in 1910, Wilbur adjusts a toy kite at Bayside, New Jersey. He brought the toy from Paris for the son of friend Frank Coffyn.

Family Affair

In 1909, the Wright family was the toast of Europe. Here, Wilbur takes sister Katharine on her first flight in Pau, France. She and other lady fliers tied down, or hobbled, their full skirts. This started a new fashion fad: the hobbled skirt.

Seeing is Believing

During a 1908 demonstration in France, Wilbur Wright flies a passenger over a country field. Two farmers watch in awe.

Off to the Races

Wright planes were showcased at the world's first air meet in Reims, France, in 1909. Flying a Wright Type A, Eugene Lefebvre rounds a pylon in a race.

Fun Fact: Lifelong Hobby

After achieving powered flight, the Wright brothers remained fascinated by kites and gliders. They glided for pleasure until Wilbur's death in 1912. He died of typhoid at age 45. Orville lived to see amazing advances in aviation. He died in 1948 at age 77.

Fun Fact: Legal Wars

The Wright brothers sued inventors who copied their idea of wing-warping with ailerons. These moveable devices on wings are still used today. They allow the pilot to bank the plane, lifting one wing while lowering the other, on turns. The courts ruled that ailerons are based on the Wrights' idea.

Aviation Takes Off

I N the decade after the Wright brothers' success, powered flight captured the world's imagination. The first international air meet was held in Reims, France in 1909. There, excited crowds watched as fliers competed for fastest speed, highest altitude, sharpest turns, and longest flight.

European plane designers now built sleeker, faster machines. Pilots vied for cash prizes offered for spanning great distances. One goal seemed nearly impossible—to cross the English Channel. Then, on July 25, 1909, Frenchman Louis Blériot took off from France in a plane of his own design. In 37 minutes, he reached England. He had become the first to cross the Channel and bridge two nations by air. A hero, he won a prize of £1,000 offered by the London *Daily Mail*.

In 1911, American Cal Rodgers flew coast to coast in an attempt to win a $50,000 prize. It was offered for the first flight across the United States in 30 days. Unfortunately, it took Rodgers 84 days to finish the long, dangerous trip.

Successful pilots were greeted much like modern sports champions or movie stars. Soon, women also joined in the thrill of taking to the skies.

▶ RACING FOR PRIZES

A poster for a French air meet features a racing Antoinette plane. As cash prizes for races grew, pilots sharpened their skills and flew longer distances. Soon, many more races were organized, spanning whole countries and even all of Europe.

▽ BLERIOT XI

This museum model shows Louis Blériot in the *XI* monoplane he flew across the English Channel. Blériot, who had no compass, wrote: "It is a strange position to be alone, unguided...over the middle of the Channel...I let the aeroplane take its own course."

GRANDE QUINZAINE
D'AVIATION
DE LA BAIE DE SEINE
LE HAVRE · TROUVILLE · DEAUVILLE

▲ LOUIS BLERIOT (1872-1936)

A postcard cartoon pictures Louis Blériot, a Frenchman who was the first to fly across the English Channel in 1909. He became world-famous for this feat, a milestone in aviation history. Blériot was among the first to try monoplanes, or single-wing planes. From Calais, France, he flew 22 miles to England, and crash-landed near the white cliffs of Dover.

▶ CRASH LANDING AT REIMS

One of many casualties, a contestant in a flying event lies upended where it crashed. This was a common occurrence for the fragile aircraft at early air shows.

◄ Harriet Quimby (1884-1912)

Harriet Quimby was the first licensed woman pilot in the United States. In 1912, she became the first woman to fly across the English Channel. She was later killed when a gust of wind overturned her plane. With no seatbelt, she fell to her death. Amazingly, the plane landed by itself!

► Flying Cross-Country

This map shows the route of Cal Rodgers, who flew from New York to California in 1911. His Wright plane, named the *Vin Fiz* for a grape drink, crashed 19 times. In a crash near the end of the 84-day trip, the pilot broke both legs and his collarbone.

◄ Glenn Curtiss (1878-1930)

Motorcycle racer Glenn Curtiss also built and flew airplanes. He became a competitor of the Wright brothers. They sued him for using ideas similar to theirs. Curtiss won the 1909 Reims speed race. His best known plane, the "Jenny," became a World War I trainer.

▼ Curtiss Hydro Plane

Glenn Curtiss taxies his invention, the Hydro plane, on water in 1911. The craft was one of the earliest seaplanes. It used ailerons, moveable wing devices, in place of the Wright brothers' wing-warping method to bank and turn the plane.

World War I: Fighters

WHEN World War I broke out in 1914, nobody thought airplanes would play an important role. Aircraft had only been invented about a decade earlier. The Germans and the Allies each had just a few hundred planes. Most could fly only about 60 to 70 miles an hour. At first, the planes were used for reconnaissance, or gathering information behind enemy lines. These planes were unarmed. Enemy pilots even waved to each other.

Yet soon, reconnaissance pilots began taking aerial photographs. These allowed military leaders to see enemy positions and plan attack strategies. Now, to chase away enemy aircraft, pilots carried guns. These early planes were called "scouts." Today, we call them "fighters."

Fighters quickly developed into weapons of war. They were built for speed and equipped with machine guns. The planes whirled after each other in duels called "dogfights." Pilots who shot down five or more planes became legendary "aces."

◄ EDDIE RICKENBACKER (1890-1973)

Captain Eddie Rickenbacker was America's highest-scoring ace in World War I. He flew only between March and April of 1918. Yet he scored 26 victories.

Before the war, Rickenbacker was a world-famous race car driver. When the United States entered the war in 1917, he trained as a pilot though he was considered old at 27. He joined and later commanded the first American squadron to fight the Germans. Rickenbacker became a famous war hero and later served as president of Eastern Airlines.

HISTORY FACT: NEW GUNS

A major help to pilots was the invention of forward-firing machine guns. They allowed pilots to aim and shoot directly through the propellers. A device called an interrupter timed the guns to fire through the spinning blades without harming them.

FUN FACT: IDENTIFICATION MARKS

Planes were marked with symbols to show which side they fought on. German planes had black crosses and Allied planes wore a roundel, a target-like emblem.

▲ THE RED BARON'S LAST FLIGHT

Closing in on a Sopwith Camel, Germany's Red Baron flies his trademark red Fokker triplane down to attack. Unknown to him, another Camel just behind him is about to open fire on him. After 80 kills, the Baron was himself shot down in April 1918.

► KNIGHTS OF THE AIR

Popular magazines of the 1920s and 1930s portrayed World War I aces as dashing heroes with glamorous lives. In reality, a fighter pilot's life was grim, dangerous, and often short. A new pilot's life expectancy averaged just three to six weeks!

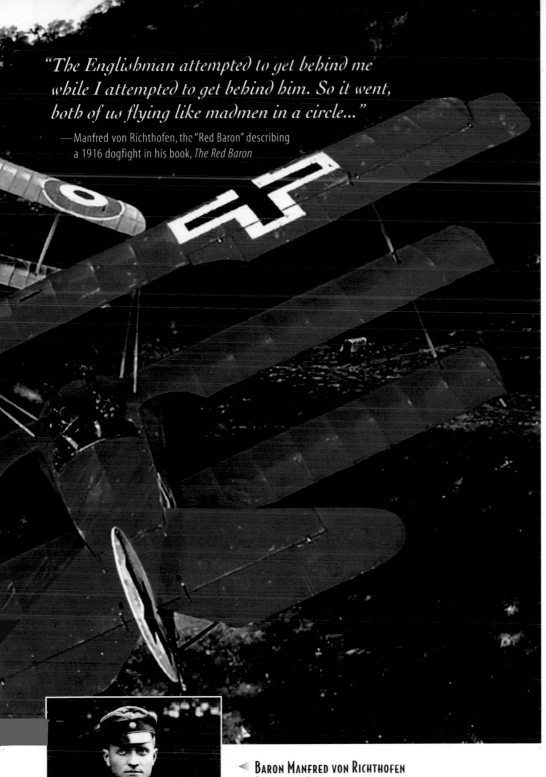

"The Englishman attempted to get behind me while I attempted to get behind him. So it went, both of us flying like madmen in a circle..."

—Manfred von Richthofen, the "Red Baron" describing a 1916 dogfight in his book, *The Red Baron*

▼ FLYING OBSERVER

To take a photograph, a reconnaissance pilot had to lean out of the side of his plane in a 70-mile-per-hour wind and snap the picture. He had to then change the plate before taking another shot.

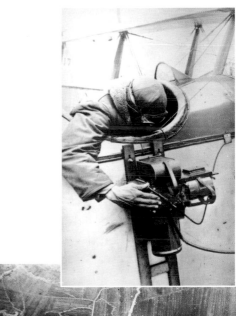

◄ BARON MANFRED VON RICHTHOFEN (1882-1918)

German Manfred von Richthofen was the highest-scoring ace of the war and one of the most famous pilots of all time. He commanded his own squadron, called the "Flying Circus" because the planes had bright colors. Richthofen's planes were brilliant red, earning him the nickname "Red Baron."

The Red Baron relished the hunt of dogfights. He had silver cups made with descriptions of each of his victims. He shot down 80 Allied planes before he himself was shot down in 1918.

CURSE YOU, RED BARON!

▲ AERIAL SPY

A French reconnaissance plane flies over enemy territory. From his vantage point, a pilot could photograph trench lines, troop locations, and arms supplies. Accurate maps were then drawn. By 1915, planes had replaced observers on horseback.

FUN FACT: CARTOON HERO

Snoopy, the world-famous "flying ace" of cartoonist Charles Schulz, continues his ongoing battle with the Red Baron. The cartoon illustrates the enduring popularity of the World War I ace legend even today.

Flying a Fighter

DURING the war, pilots developed expert skill at dogfighting. And aircraft companies turned out faster, more agile planes. By the war's end, fighter planes could fly 130 miles an hour and climb to over 20,000 feet. Climbing high allowed faster attack speed in diving. Both German and Allied pilots developed dogfight strategies: surprising an enemy by diving from above, sneaking up from behind, or attacking from the sun, hidden by the glare.

Flying a fighter was difficult and often dangerous. A wonderful plane in expert hands, the British Sopwith Camel was tricky to fly. It killed many student pilots because its engine tended to suddenly cut off. Pilots called their planes "flaming coffins" because of the danger of fire. A bullet hitting the gas tank behind the pilot's seat could trigger an explosion and engulf the wood-and-fabric plane in flames. Pilots could not bail out, because at the time they had no parachutes!

◄ Flight Dress
Pilots in open cockpits needed warm clothing at high altitudes. American pilot Edmund Genet stands beside his plane in France. He wears a fur-lined suit, warm boots, and leather helmet. Goggles protect his eyes from icy winds and oil sprayed out by the engine.

► Sopwith Camel
The British Sopwith Camel was one of the most successful fighters of World War I. Quick and highly maneuverable, it was a supreme performer in dogfights. Camels shot down over 1,290 German aircraft, more than any other Allied plane.

Fun Fact: Flying Scarf
The silk scarf many pilots wore became a famous symbol of brave flying aces. However, it was not originally worn for style, but to keep warm in the freezing air aloft. It was also a handy "windshield wiper" for the pilot's goggles.

▼ Controlling the Plane
Unlike driving a car, flying a plane requires control in three dimensions, or axes: they are called pitch, yaw, and roll. To control the plane's **roll**, or rotating motion, the pilot moves wing devices called ailerons in opposite directions. The pilot moves an elevator stick to control **pitch**, the up-and-down movement of the airplane's nose. Moving the rudder in the plane's tail controls the right and left turning motion, called **yaw**.

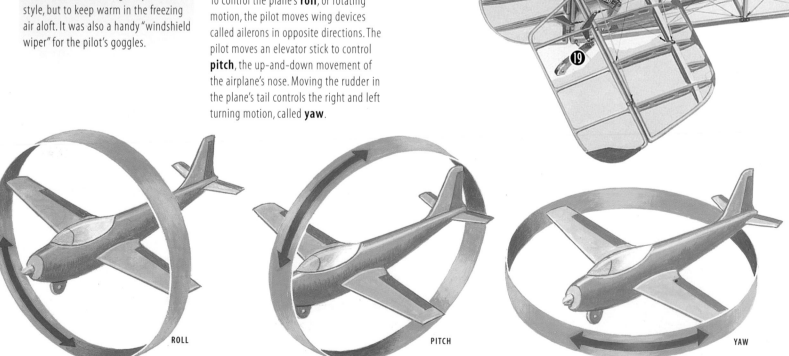

ROLL   PITCH   YAW

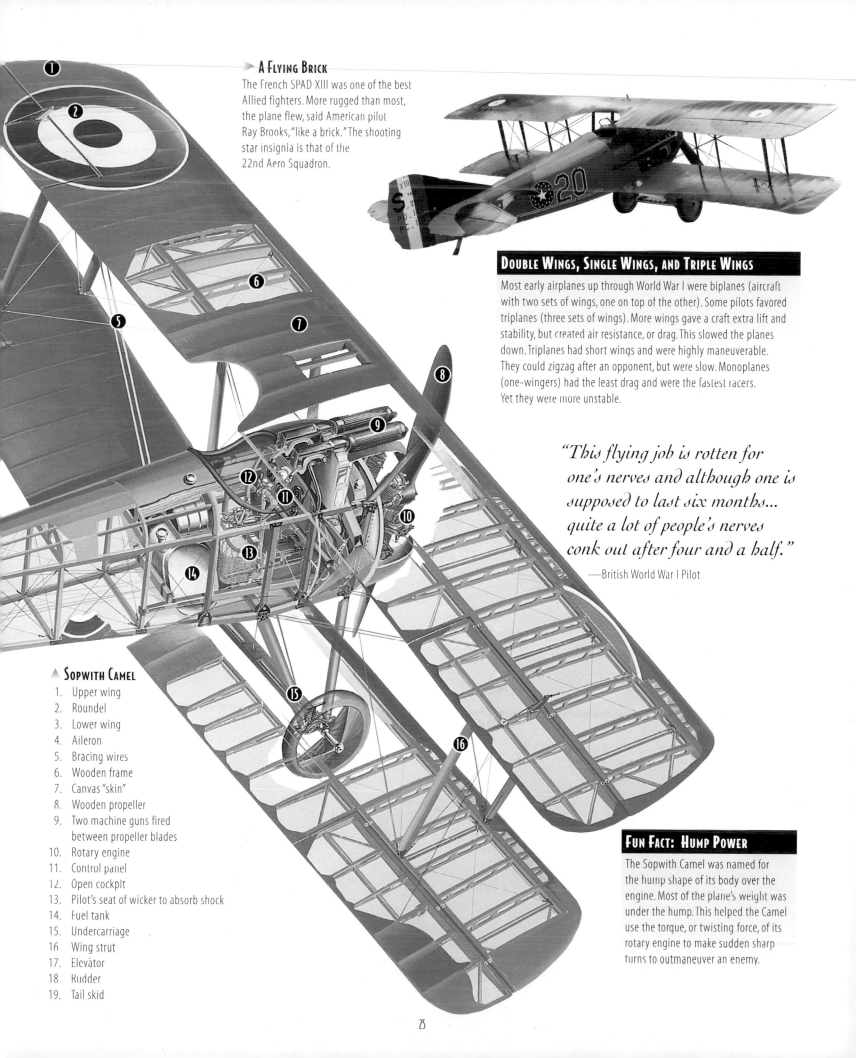

A Flying Brick

The French SPAD XIII was one of the best Allied fighters. More rugged than most, the plane flew, said American pilot Ray Brooks, "like a brick." The shooting star insignia is that of the 22nd Aero Squadron.

Double Wings, Single Wings, and Triple Wings

Most early airplanes up through World War I were biplanes (aircraft with two sets of wings, one on top of the other). Some pilots favored triplanes (three sets of wings). More wings gave a craft extra lift and stability, but created air resistance, or drag. This slowed the planes down. Triplanes had short wings and were highly maneuverable. They could zigzag after an opponent, but were slow. Monoplanes (one-wingers) had the least drag and were the fastest racers. Yet they were more unstable.

"This flying job is rotten for one's nerves and although one is supposed to last six months... quite a lot of people's nerves conk out after four and a half."

—British World War I Pilot

Sopwith Camel

1. Upper wing
2. Roundel
3. Lower wing
4. Aileron
5. Bracing wires
6. Wooden frame
7. Canvas "skin"
8. Wooden propeller
9. Two machine guns fired between propeller blades
10. Rotary engine
11. Control panel
12. Open cockpit
13. Pilot's seat of wicker to absorb shock
14. Fuel tank
15. Undercarriage
16. Wing strut
17. Elevator
18. Rudder
19. Tail skid

Fun Fact: Hump Power

The Sopwith Camel was named for the hump shape of its body over the engine. Most of the plane's weight was under the hump. This helped the Camel use the torque, or twisting force, of its rotary engine to make sudden sharp turns to outmaneuver an enemy.

World War I: Bombers

I N the early days of the war, there were no specialized bombers. Pilots simply dropped small bombs and grenades from their cockpits. But by 1915, Germany was sending a new fleet of 30 giant airships, called Zeppelins, to bomb England. Named for their designer, Count Ferdinand von Zeppelin, these enormous airships filled with hydrogen stretched over 640 feet long. They could stay up several days and carry many tons of bombs.

Looming over the English landscape, the Zeppelins terrorized the people. They destroyed homes and killed hundreds of civilians. Yet they were vulnerable to British fighter planes, which shot them down with incendiary, or explosive, bullets.

By 1917, both sides were building fast, powerful bomber airplanes. The Germans built Gotha bombers, which bombed London day and night, and the gigantic Zeppelin Staaken R.IV. It could carry bombs as big as 2,200 pounds. German planes dropped 280 tons of bombs over England. The bomber had become one of the most destructive of all instruments of war.

▲ GERMAN GIANT
The Zeppelin Staaken R.IV was the biggest bomber of the war. Its wingspan of 138 feet was just a few feet shorter than a World War II B-29. Its seven-man crew included two pilots, two mechanics, a navigator, a radio operator, and a fuel attendant.

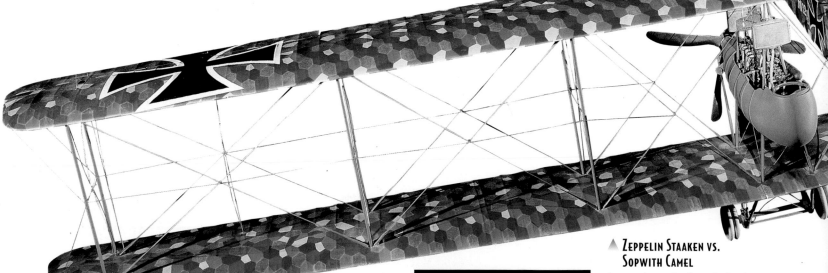

HISTORY FACT: MEGA-BOMBER
The Germans planned, but never built, an even bigger triplane bomber with a wingspan of nearly 170 feet! It was to be a transatlantic warplane that could attack the United States.

▲ ZEPPELIN STAAKEN VS. SOPWITH CAMEL
Germany's massive Zeppelin Staaken bomber made many night-bombing raids on England. This model from the Museum's collection is painted in a German camouflage pattern. A model of an attacking Sopwith Camel night fighter in the same scale (top) gives an idea of the bomber's size.

◀ ◀ ATTACKING THE MONSTER

British fighters attack a huge Zeppelin airship (far left) returning after a bombing raid on England. Damaged and smoking from the fighters' gunfire, the Zeppelin will escape by climbing high.

◀ INSIDE A ZEPPELIN

In the engine gondola of a Zeppelin (above), crew members operate the engines as a machine gunner watches for enemy fighters. In the control gondola (left), an officer gives orders to crew manning control wheels.

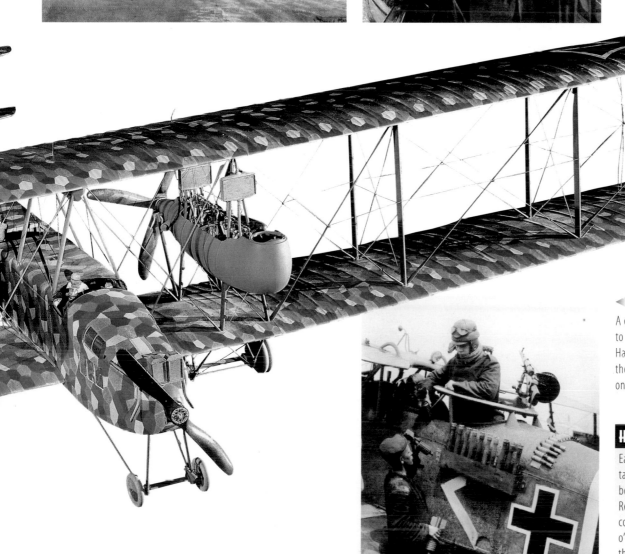

◀ HAND BOMBING

A crewman passes small hand bombs to the pilot in the cockpit of a German Halberstadt fighter. The pilot will drop the bombs by hand from the air. A box on the plane's side holds hand grenades.

HISTORY FACT: ZEROING IN

Early bombers often missed their targets because the planes had no bombsights to aim bombs. Reconnaissance pilots devised a clock code to pinpoint an enemy. Twelve o'clock was north, six o'clock south, three east, and nine west. This code has been used by fighter pilots ever since.

Barnstorming

AFTER the war ended in 1918, thousands of military planes were available at cheap prices. The most common plane, the Curtiss JN-4, was called the "Jenny." It had been used as a pilot trainer. Many war pilots, now out of work, wanted to keep flying. They bought surplus planes and traveled the countryside as entertainers. Alone or in troupes, they gave shows in farm fields, sleeping in barns or by their planes.

Called barnstormers, these fliers thrilled audiences with daring displays. They performed flying acrobatics with loops, spins, rolls, and dizzying dives. Some did stunt flying. They performed tricks on the wings of a flying plane or hung upside-down from the plane wheels. Some even hung by their teeth. In one stunt, two pilots flew their planes side by side, locked controls, and scrambled over the wings to change places! Pilots often gave rides to people for money or a meal. Many women, as well as men, became famous barnstormers.

Fun Fact: Storming Barns

Barnstormers got their name from the theatrical tradition of performers doing traveling shows in barns.

▼ Plane for Sale

Surplus military airplanes like this De Havilland DH-4 were good bargains after World War I. Worth thousands of dollars during wartime, they might cost just a few hundred dollars after the war.

▲ Bessie Coleman (1892-1926)

Bessie Coleman was the first African-American woman pilot. She got her pilot's license in France in 1921, and worked as a barnstormer in the United States. She became famous as "Queen Bess, Daredevil Aviatrix." Bessie dreamed of starting her own flying school and once said, "You have never lived until you have flown." She was killed in an accident during a practice parachute jump.

▶ FLYING CIRCUS

A poster for Freddie Lund's Air Circus announces an upcoming show at a local airport. This traveling troupe featured stunts in a 1910 biplane and parachute jumps from a "looping glider."

◀ WINGING IT

A young wingwalker braces to leap from one plane to another during a 1926 barnstorming show. Above, one daredevil hangs from the plane's axle while another stands over the plane's tail. Below left, stunt flier Jersey Ringel performs gymnastics under the wing.

▼ TRAVEL FUN

In the 1920s, some airplanes were promoted as fast, fun ways to travel. Here, swimsuited bathing beauties pose with the crew of the "Buckeye," a converted World War I Navy flying boat. It ferried summer vacationers across Lake Erie in 1922 and 1923.

▶ PILOT PAL

Pilot Edmund Poillot and a canine companion get ready for takeoff in a Voisin biplane. Many early fliers took along pet mascots. In the cold air aloft, a warm, furry friend was doggone comforting.

FUN FACT: RIDE REQUEST

As a young man, Charles Lindbergh was a barnstormer. Once after a show, an old lady came up and asked him: "Mister, how much would it cost to fly me up to Heaven and leave me there?"

Racing for the Skies

THE years between World War I and World War II are often called the Golden Age of Aviation. During this time people believed anything was possible. Designers worked constantly to build better performing planes. Fliers pushed the limits of flying. They set new records for distance, speed, duration, and altitude. In this period, many famous air races were established. Pilots competed for trophies, prize money, and the glory of conquering the skies.

The National Air Races in the United States drew huge crowds in the 1930s. Famous races included the 50-mile speed race for the Thompson Trophy and the long-distance, cross-country race for the Bendix Trophy. The Schneider Trophy race, a competition for seaplanes, was held from 1913 to 1938. France won the first Schneider Trophy in 1913 with an average speed of 46 miles an hour. In 1931, a British plane won. Its average speed—340 miles an hour—shows how far airplanes had come.

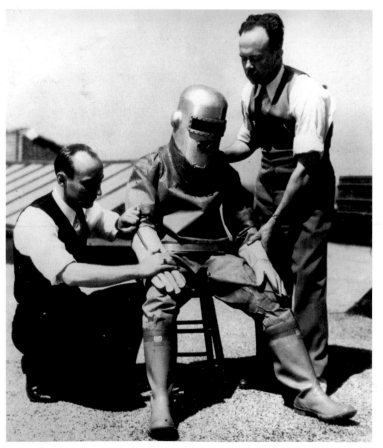

◀ WILEY POST (1899-1935)

Wiley Post became the first person to fly solo around the world in 1933. He also set early altitude records and designed the first pressure suit. Here, Post wears an early design of his suit, adapted from a deep-sea diver's outfit. It supplied oxygen from a tube to the helmet and allowed Post to reach heights of nearly 55,000 feet. He proved that flying in the jet stream, a high, fast-flowing river of air, could increase a plane's speed. Post died in a crash in 1935 with his friend, humorist Will Rogers.

Winnie Mae

Wiley Post set two round-the-world records in his Lockheed Vega, *Winnie Mae*. This painting shows the *Winnie Mae* carrying Post and a navigator over the Volga River in 1931. They circled the globe in 8 days and 15 hours. In 1933, Post flew the 15,596-mile trip solo in 7 days and 19 hours.

Bendix Trophy

One of the top racing prizes, the Bendix Trophy was first awarded in 1931. It was given to the winner of the Bendix Transcontinental Race between Los Angeles and Cleveland.

Racing Souvenirs

Mementos from the Museum collection recall the era of early air races. They include a poster for the 1932 National Air Races, an advertisement for the 1928 Schneider Trophy seaplane race, and a ticket to the 1929 National Air Races.

James H. "Jimmy" Doolittle (1896-1993)

A famous flier of the Golden Age, Army Lieutenant Jimmy Doolittle served in World War I as a flight instructor. In 1929, he became the first pilot to fly "blind," using only instruments to take off, fly, and land. A top racing pilot, Doolittle won the 1925 Schneider Trophy in a U.S. Army float plane (above). In 1931, he won the Bendix transcontinental air race. The next year, Doolittle set a world record of 294 miles an hour when he flew a Gee Bee race plane and won the Thompson Trophy.

Douglas World Cruisers

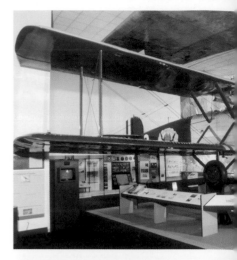

ONE of the most famous early distance flights was that of the Douglas World Cruisers in 1924. They were the first planes ever to go around the globe. Built for the U.S. Army Air Service, the World Cruisers were open-cockpit biplanes. They had landing gear that could be changed from wheels to floats so the craft could land on water or ground. Named for four cities, the planes were the *Boston*, *Chicago*, *New Orleans*, and *Seattle*.

On April 6, 1924, the four planes with two-man crews took off from Seattle, Washington. They were to fly west over Alaska, around Asia, across the North Atlantic, and back across the United States. On the trip, the *Seattle* crashed in Alaska and the *Boston* went down in the North Atlantic. Only the *Chicago* and the *New Orleans* completed the flight, traveling through 29 countries. After six months they returned to Seattle, ending the incredible 26,345-mile journey.

 ### Good Luck Charm

A toy monkey named "Maggie" (left) rode in the Douglas World Cruiser *Chicago* on its long journey. The plane's open cockpit (below) had few instruments, but a big steering wheel to control ailerons and elevators. Leather trim was to protect the pilot in a possible crash.

FUN FACT: REPAIR WORK

Changing all the World Cruisers' pontoons for wheels during the trip took three days. Changing the planes' engines also took three days. The two surviving planes used nine engines each.

The *Chicago*

One of the two surviving World Cruisers, the *Chicago* is in the National Air and Space Museum. The two-seat biplane carried a crew of two, a pilot and a mechanic. It had no radio, radar, or weather instruments to help make the long round-the-world flight.

Resting at Anchor

The diorama below, in the Museum collection, depicts the World Cruisers refueling in Seward, Alaska. At right, the planes sit on their pontoon floats, anchored off Sitka, Alaska. Soon after, the *Seattle* crashed into a mountain in fog.

Going the Distance

THROUGHOUT the 1920s and 1930s, pilots competed to set new distance records as well as endurance records–staying the longest time in the air. In 1923, a Fokker T-2 Army transport plane made the first nonstop flight across the United States. Army Air Service Lieutenants Oakley G. Kelly and John A. Macready piloted the T-2 from New York to San Diego. The trip took 26 hours and 50 minutes. Along the way, people listened eagerly for the plane and watched for it in the sky. When the T-2 landed, a huge crowd cheered the landmark flight.

In 1929, the crew of a tri-motor Fokker, the *Question Mark*, set an endurance record of 150 hours, 40 minutes, and 15 seconds in the air. They flew over California, covering 11,000 miles. The flight required midair refueling from another plane, using a 40-foot hose.

An astonishing record for sustained flight was set in 1936 by the Curtiss Robin *Ole Miss*. The pilots, brothers Fred and Algene Key, took off from Meridian, Mississippi on June 4 and landed July 1 after 653 hours–27 days in the air! The plane received food and fuel in over 400 contacts with another plane. Such flights increased the public's confidence in aircraft.

▲ Risky Business

Pilot Fred Key services the engine of the Curtiss Robin *Ole Miss* by climbing on a special catwalk. During the record flight of 27 days, the two pilots took turns sleeping on top of a fuel tank.

▶ Filling up in Flight

During its 1929 flight, the *Question Mark* gets fuel from another plane by a hose. This was dangerous, since a drop of gas leaking on a hot engine could ignite and blow up the plane. Left, a Boeing PW-9D "blackboard plane" carried messages to the *Question Mark* crew.

MOON HAD TROUBLE WITH HOSE — HE HAS GAS THIS TRIP

► Fokker T-2

The Fokker T-2, now in the Museum, made the first nonstop flight across the United States in 1923. At right, pilots John Macready, left, and Oakley Kelly stand with the 737 gallons of gas and 40 gallons of oil used for the flight.

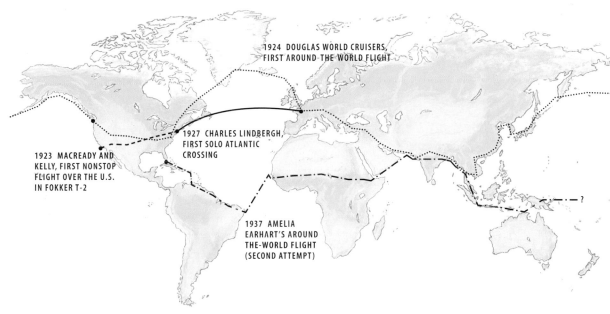

1924 DOUGLAS WORLD CRUISERS, FIRST AROUND THE WORLD FLIGHT

1927 CHARLES LINDBERGH, FIRST SOLO ATLANTIC CROSSING

1923 MACREADY AND KELLY, FIRST NONSTOP FLIGHT OVER THE U.S. IN FOKKER T-2

1937 AMELIA EARHART'S AROUND THE-WORLD FLIGHT (SECOND ATTEMPT)

▲ Record Distance Flights

Routes shown here trace four of the most famous flights of the 1920s and 1930s.

► Flight Crew

The crew of the *Question Mark* includes (left to right) Major Carl Spaatz, in command, chief pilot Ira Eaker, Harry Halverson, Lieutenant Elwood Quesada, and Sergeant Roy Hooe, chief mechanic.

FUN FACT: TRICKY REPAIR

During the flight of the Fokker T-2 pilot Kelly had to disassemble and repair a faulty voltage regulator as his co-pilot controlled the plane from the rear seat.

Charles Lindbergh

"Here all around me, is the Atlantic—its expanse, its depth, its power, its wild and open water... If my plane can stay aloft, if my engine can keep on running, then so can I."

—Charles Lindbergh, *The Spirit of St. Louis*

O N May 20, 1927, 25-year-old Charles Lindbergh took off from New York on one of history's most famous flights. An unknown mail pilot, he hoped to win a $25,000 prize by being first to fly nonstop from New York to Paris. He would fly 3,610 miles–alone. Six other pilots had died trying.

Heavily laden with fuel, Lindbergh's monoplane, the *Spirit of St. Louis*, barely got off the ground. Lindbergh had not slept in 24 hours. But because the weather was clearing, he set off. To avoid extra weight, he carried no radio, relying only on his instruments and navigational skills. At times he flew in total darkness, except for the eerie glow of his instruments. On the difficult crossing, Lindbergh battled terrifying storms, fog, cold, and worst of all, sleep. He wrote, "I've lost command of my eyelids. They shut...stick tight as though with glue..I've *got* to find a way to stay alert. There's no alternative but death and failure." His flight lasted 33½ hours. Landing in Paris, he became an instant hero.

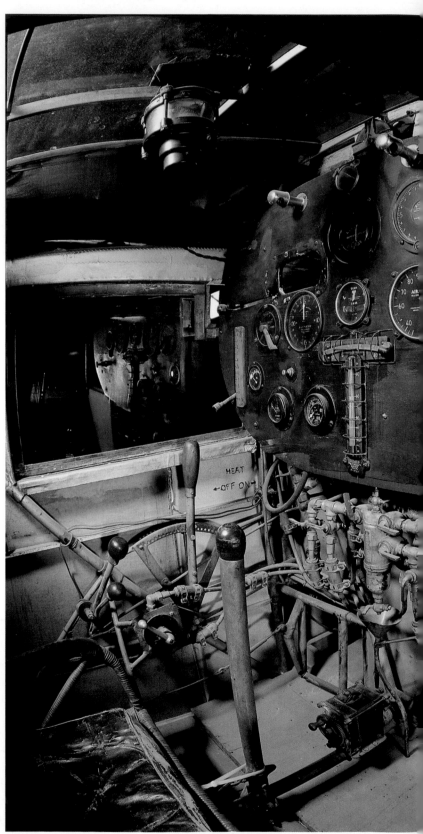

▲ "The Lone Eagle"
Charles Lindbergh became the most famous aviator of his day. His courage, daring, and sheer endurance at achieving the solo flight won public admiration and acclaim. Lindbergh did much to inspire people's faith in the airplane.

▶ In the Cockpit
The *Spirit*'s cramped cockpit, squeezed in behind a fuel tank, had no forward window. Lindbergh used a periscope or turned the plane to look out the side windows. Instruments include a T-shaped altimeter to measure altitude.

◄ THE *SPIRIT OF ST. LOUIS*

Charles Lindbergh's famous airplane now hangs in the National Air and Space Museum. The sturdy monoplane was built with extra tanks to hold 450 gallons of fuel for the Atlantic flight. It carried Lindbergh into history May 20-21, 1927.

◄ NOSE ART

Flags of many nations decorate the *Spirit* near the Wright J-5 Whirlwind engine circling the plane's nose. The flags represent countries Lindbergh visited on a goodwill tour of Latin America and the Caribbean after his Atlantic flight.

▼ FAME AND FORTUNE

The *Spirit of St. Louis* takes off on a national tour (bottom) following Lindbergh's Atlantic flight. A check for $25,000 (below) was presented to Lindbergh as his prize for making the first nonstop flight between New York and Paris.

FUN FACT: TRAVELING LIGHT

Charles Lindbergh took just two canteens of water and a bag of sandwiches to eat on his long flight. When he landed in Paris, he had been awake 57½ hours!

Amelia Earhart

AMELIA Earhart was the most famous woman pilot of her time. Adventurous and fearless, she pushed herself to the limits, setting many new records. On May 20, 1932, five years to the day after Lindbergh's Atlantic crossing, Amelia took off to fly solo across the Atlantic. In her bright red Lockheed Vega, she left Newfoundland and landed nearly 15 hours later in Londonderry, Ireland. During the trip, her altimeter, which measured her altitude, failed. She encountered violent storms, icing on her wings, and a sudden downward drop of 3,000 feet! Yet she managed to pull the plane up, and never lost her nerve. She became the first woman to make the solo crossing.

In 1937, Amelia took off with a navigator for her most ambitious goal—a round-the-world flight in her new Lockheed Electra. Flying back home over the Pacific, the Electra mysteriously disappeared. No trace of Amelia, her navigator, or her plane was ever found.

▲ Proud Pilot

Amelia Earhart poses happily with her new Lockheed Electra 10E (above). In this plane, she attempted a round-the-world flight that ended with her disappearance in 1937. At left, fans greet Amelia in Ireland after her flight across the Atlantic in her red Lockheed Vega in 1932.

◄ FLYING SUPERSTAR

Thousands of admirers flock around Amelia after her landing in Oakland, California, in 1935 in another Vega. She had just made the first solo flight from Hawaii to the mainland and was a worldwide celebrity.

"Please know I am quite aware of the hazards. I want to do it because I want to do it. Women must try to do things as men have tried."

Amelia Earhart

HISTORY FACT: MYSTERIOUS LOSS

When Amelia's plane vanished over the Pacific in 1937, a huge search by ships and aircraft failed to find her. No one knows her fate. Yet many experts think she lost her way, ran out of fuel, and crashed into the ocean.

◄ FLIGHT CHECK

Before her round-the-world flight, Amelia takes a final look at the Electra with mechanics. After her flight, she planned to use the Electra as a "flying laboratory" for aviation research.

► FAMOUS AIRPLANE

Amelia's red Vega is today in the National Air and Space Museum. One of the most advanced planes of its time, the Vega had a streamlined wood fuselage, molded plywood "skin," and internally braced wings.

FUN FACT: HONORED FLIER

Amelia Earhart was showered with honors for her solo Atlantic flight. She received many awards, including the Distinguished Flying Cross and the National Geographic Society's Special Gold Medal.

Airmail to Airlines

AIRMAIL service began in the United States in 1918. The U.S. Post Office bought military biplanes, such as the Curtiss Jenny, and renovated them to carry mail. Pilots flew the planes in relays like the Pony Express, carrying mail coast to coast. In 1921, seven planes flew the San Francisco mail to New York in 33 hours, compared to 108 hours required by trains.

Flying mail was difficult and deadly dangerous. Pilots crossed treacherous mountains. They flew at night with no landing lights. In open cockpits they endured temperatures of 40 degrees below zero, driving rain, and blinding snowstorms. Planes broke down often. One pilot's control stick broke off in his hand! By 1925, thirty-one airmail pilots had died in crashes.

Private companies then took over flying the mail and carrying passengers. They designed planes to attract more passengers. Among the first successes were the Ford Tri-Motor and the Boeing 247D. These planes inspired great public trust and led to commercial airlines.

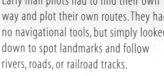

◀ Via Airmail
Early advertisements and a shipping label from the Museum collection promote airmail service in the 1920s and 1930s.

▲ ▲ Airmail Pilots
Rugged airmail pilots (top) pose for a January 1922 portrait. For warmth, they wore two pairs of socks, underwear, and gloves, as well as sweaters, fur-lined suits, and scarves. So bundled up, many had to be lifted into their cockpits.

FUN FACTS: GETTING THERE
Early mail pilots had to find their own way and plot their own routes. They had no navigational tools, but simply looked down to spot landmarks and follow rivers, roads, or railroad tracks.

▲ Douglas M-2
The Douglas M-2 was an early airmail plane. It flew from Los Angeles to Salt Lake City from 1926 to 1930. Mannequins represent the pilot and mail workers in this Museum display. Occasionally, a passenger would squeeze in to ride with the mail.

Ford Tri-Motor

The Ford Tri-Motor, made by Henry Ford in 1926, was a popular early airliner. Noisy but reliable, it seated 13 passengers. Its all-metal body and three engines made people feel safer. It was known as the "Tin Goose."

Boeing 247D

First built in 1934, the Boeing 247D was used by United Airlines. Sleek and comfortable, it cruised at 189 miles an hour. Now in the Museum, this plane was flown in the 1934 London-to-Melbourne MacRobertson Air Race (see map above). It came in third.

Racing Star

Roscoe Turner, the most famous and colorful racing pilot of the 1930s, shows off his pet lion, Gilmore. Gilmore often flew along with Turner. In 1934, Turner piloted the Boeing 247D airliner above in the MacRobertson Race.

FUN FACT: FLYING PETS

Many early pilots flew with unusual pets. One pilot had a 109-pound black Idaho wolf named "Ace." Another had a squirrel that loved to fly. It rode in the pilot's top coat pocket or clung to his scarf.

Air Transport

ARLY passenger flights of the 1920s were rough. Planes had no heat or air conditioning. They were not pressurized and usually could not fly over storms. They pitched and bucked in turbulence, and passengers were very airsick. In 1930, the first stewardesses, all nurses, were hired. Among the first rules they had to learn was: make sure passengers who want to use the restroom don't walk out the exit door!

Commercial air transportation grew rapidly during the 1930s and early 1940s. The Boeing 247D was the first modern airliner, with comfortable seats and air conditioning. Yet it could only seat 10 passengers. Many airlines asked builders to design a bigger plane. The result was the Douglas DC-3, which began service in 1936. It could seat up to 32 passengers. Fast, comfortable, and dependable, the DC-3 was the first passenger aircraft to make a profit without carrying mail. By 1939, ninety percent of airline passengers worldwide were flown in DC-3s.

▼ Flight Attendants

United Airlines stewardesses pose with a Boeing 247D. First serving as nurses, stewardesses later served meals and kept passengers safe and comfortable. These stewardess airline wings and identification badge are from the Museum collection.

▲ Worldwide Travel

The Douglas DC-3 (above) became the world's most successful airliner, flying cheaper, safer, and faster than competitors. Over 1,000 are still flying. By the 1930s, planes were taking people around the globe, as shown in these Museum advertisements.

▲ Comfortable Ride

In an American Airlines DC-7 of the 1940s, passengers enjoy chatting and relaxing in the plane's spacious Sky Lounge.

◄ In the Pilot's Seat

A pilot and co-pilot sit at the controls of a DC-3. The cockpit had two sets of instruments and an autopilot. Pilots said the DC-3 handled so easily, it practically flew itself. The plane could reach speeds up to 230 miles an hour.

Airships

During World War I, German airships were used for long-range bombing raids over England. Their ability to fly quickly over great distances led to a golden age of passenger airships in the 1920s and 1930s. Two huge German ships, the *Graf Zeppelin* and the *Hindenburg*, carried passengers over the Atlantic.

Driven by diesel engines, the airships could cross the ocean in about two days, much faster than a ship. The airships were like flying luxury hotels. They included private cabins, observation decks, fine dining rooms, and lounges. The trip was so comfortable one passenger described it as "being carried in the arms of angels."

The *Hindenburg*, over 800 feet long, was the largest airship ever built. Passengers and crew occupied a small part of the ship. Most of it was filled with gas cells that held hydrogen, the flammable gas that gave the ship its lift. In 1937, the *Hindenburg* exploded and crashed. The tragedy ended the age of passenger airships.

IN 2 DAYS TO NORTH AMERICA!
DEUTSCHE ZEPPELIN-REEDEREI

▲ The *Hindenburg*
This poster advertises the *Hindenburg*. Measuring 804 feet long, the airship was just 78 feet shorter than the *Titanic*. It could carry 72 passengers and travel 80 miles an hour. Huge gas cells inside its metal-and-fabric frame held 7,062,100 cubic feet of hydrogen.

▲ Graf Zeppelin
The German airship *Graf Zeppelin* floats over a Dornier Do-X flying boat. The *Graf Zeppelin* was the *Hindenburg*'s sister ship. The two luxury airships carried thousands of passengers over the Atlantic between World Wars I and II.

▶ Lap of Luxury
On an airship's promenade deck (top right), passengers relaxed and enjoyed breathtaking views out the window. In the dining room of the *Hindenburg* (right), stewards served passengers wine and gourmet meals from the galley.

FUN FACT: NOT CHEAP

During the 1920s, only the rich could afford airship travel. A one-way trip over the Atlantic could cost as much as a new car. A round-trip fare could equal the cost of a moderate house.

▼ HINDENBURG CRASH

On May 6, 1937, the *Hindenburg* was approaching Lakehurst, New Jersey. It suddenly exploded, burst into flames, and fell from the sky. Of the 97 on board, 35 died. No one knows for sure what triggered the explosion.

HISTORY FACT: BETTER GAS

Airships like the *Hindenburg* were prone to explosions because hydrogen, the gas that kept the ship up, was flammable. Today, airships use helium, a gas that does not burn.

Flying Boats

I N the 1930s, flying boats became the largest, most comfortable passenger planes in the world. The spacious planes had hulls shaped like boats and floats under their wings. They could land and take off on the sea, as well as lakes and rivers. In a time when aircraft engines were still unreliable, people thought flying boats were a safer way to travel over the ocean.

Pan American Airlines called its flying boats clippers, after the speedy sailing ships. They carried passengers to exotic destinations, such as the Far East and South America, at a time when few airports existed.

Flying boats were luxury craft designed to compete with ocean liners. The biggest was Pan Am's Boeing 314 Clipper. A 106-foot-long-giant, it carried passengers at 174 miles an hour to Hong Kong or other cites in unequaled comfort. Yet as airports were built all over the world, flying boats were replaced by land aircraft.

ATLANTIC CLIPPER
PILOTS STATION
FLIGHT CONTROL DECK
PAN AMERICAN WORLD AIRWA
FIRST COMPARTMENT
GALLEY
THIRD COMPARTMENT

FUN FACT: SHIP-SHAPE

When a flying boat landed on water, it tied up at a mooring buoy or simply dropped its own anchor, like a ship.

▲ BOEING 314 CLIPPER

A model made by the Boeing Company in 1939 shows the interior of the Boeing 314 Clipper. The 106-foot-long flying boat carried 74 passengers. It had a dining room, bar, deluxe suite, and cabins with 40 night-sleeping berths.

◀ Traveling the World

The cover of a 1930s Pan American timetable, in the Museum collection, shows routes spanning much of the globe. These routes opened the world to air travelers.

▼ China Clipper

The Martin M-130, the "China Clipper," rests at a mooring station off Manila after her first transpacific flight on November 29, 1935. The streamlined plane flew from San Francisco to Manila in 59 hours.

PAN AMERICAN MAKES THE WORLD *SMALLER*

BAGGAGE COMPARTMENT   WOMEN'S POWDER ROOM

FOURTH COMPARTMENT   SIXTH COMPARTMENT   SUITE DE LUXE

▶ Bermuda by Air

A 1937 baggage label advertises a Pan Am flight from New York to Bermuda in five hours.

BERMUDA BY AIR in 5 HOURS via PAN AMERICAN AIRWAYS

World War II: Fighters

ERY different from the flimsy biplanes of World War I, the fighter aircraft of World War II were tough, fast, and efficient. Aircraft had now become a primary means of waging war. Two nations, Germany and Japan, set out to dominate the world. In 1939, Nazi Germany began invading European countries. The German air force was called the Luftwaffe, or "air weapon." Its Messerschmitt Bf 109 was a swift, fearsome fighter. More than 33,000 were produced.

German fighters and bombers terrorized Europe. Allied nations, including the United States, produced thousands of aircraft to fight Germany and Japan. Fighters escorted bombers deep into enemy territory and battled in dogfights. Pilot skill was paramount. Spurred by war, aircraft advanced rapidly. Sleek new fighters flew at over 400 miles an hour and went 2,000 miles without refueling. By war's end, the first experimental jet fighters would be in the air.

▲ **BENJAMIN O. DAVIS, JR., (1912-   )**
Benjamin O. Davis was the commander of four squadrons of black aviators in World War II. The first African-American fighter pilots, they have come to be known as the Tuskegee Airmen. They flew P-51 Mustangs and were best known for escorting bombers. Davis ordered the pilots to stay close to the bombers, and not one was lost to enemy fire.

▼ **FAMOUS AIRMEN**
Five pilots of the 332nd Fighter Group pose with *Skipper's Darlin'*, one of the North American P-51 Mustangs they flew in Europe.

"If I come through the war in one piece, I'll always be glad I was able to handle one of the tough jobs."

—Quentin C. Aanenson,
U.S. Fighter Pilot, October 1944

▲ **COMBAT PILOT**
Wounded and dazed, pilot Quentin C. Aanenson poses with his P-47 Thunderbolt fighter plane, *Topsy*. Aanenson had just crash-landed on his base after being hit by "flak," or antiaircraft fire, in a mission over Germany.

Supermarine Spitfire

Britain's most famous fighter, the Spitfire was fast and nimble and could outmaneuver the German Bf 109. This Spitfire in the Museum is a high-altitude version of the fighter, and could fly over 40,000 feet.

▲ Mitsubishi Zero

Light and quick, this Japanese fighter was a tough opponent. It fought in every Pacific action, including the Japanese attack on Pearl Harbor in 1941.

▼ Curtiss P-40 Warhawk

Lieutenant Donald Lopez stands with his P-40 Warhawk in 1943. Now Deputy Director of the National Air and Space Museum, Lopez became an ace flying with the Fourteenth Air Force. They battled the Japanese in China.

▲ North American P-51 Mustang

A pilot smiles inside his P-51 D Mustang. This U.S. fighter could fly at 440 miles an hour. It was fitted with a drop tank so it could fly extra miles to go deep inside Germany. Swastikas on the plane's side represent German planes shot down.

➤ Messerschmitt Bf 109

Germany's Messerschmitt Bf 109 was the main opponent of the P-51 Mustang and the British Spitfire. With a top speed of 385 miles an hour, it could swiftly climb, dive, and turn in dogfights.

World War II: Battle of Britain

N 1940, after conquering France, German leader
Adolf Hitler decided to invade Great Britain.
The first step was to destroy the RAF, Britain's
Royal Air Force. This led to one of the most
famous air battles in history. In summer of 1940,
the Luftwaffe sent waves of aircraft over the
English Channel. At first, the RAF had fewer
than 700 fighters to face over 1,500 incoming
German bombers and fighters! Yet Britain had
advance warning of the intruders from radar
along its coast. It was also producing 400 new
fighter planes a month.

The RAF Spitfire and German
Messerschmitt fighters fought furious dogfights
in the skies as the British people watched.
Spitfires attacked Messerschmitts guarding
bombers. Hurricane fighters then attacked the
bombers. In spite of night bombing of London,
called "the Blitz," the Luftwaffe found it could
not crush the RAF or the British spirit. Germany
suffered heavy plane losses, and finally withdrew.
By winning this battle in the air, the British
prevented the German invasion.

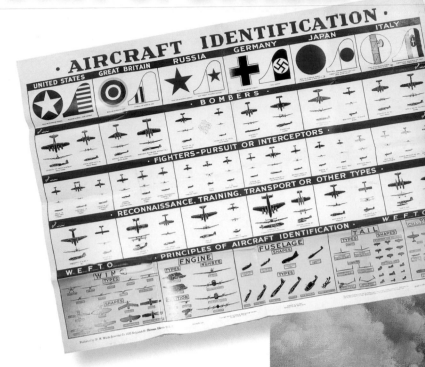

▼ Scramble!

British fighter pilots run to their Hawker
Hurricane fighters to take off during the
Battle of Britain. Though not as agile as
the Spitfire, the sturdy Hurricane easily
shot down large numbers of slower,
low-flying German bombers.

◄ OBSERVER CORPS

British men and women volunteered as aircraft spotters in 1940. This chart shows how to identify various planes. Many Allies fought with the RAF. The poster at right helped recruit pilots for the Royal Australian Air Force.

FUN FACT: SUPER BINOCULARS

During the Battle of Britain, the British relied on their coastal radar, called the Chain Home system. It could detect German planes 40 miles away. German pilots called this new radar "super binoculars."

▼ "ACHTUNG, SPITFIRE!"

German pilots warn each other as a Spitfire zooms in to attack. The agile "Spit" could quickly train its 8 machine guns in a deadly hail of bullets and tear apart an enemy 300 yards away.

This is a Man's job!

Join the

R·A·A·F

ENQUIRE AT COUNCIL CHAMBERS

"Never...was so much owed by so many to so few. All hearts go out to the fighter pilots, whose brilliant actions we see with our own eyes day after day..."

—British Prime Minister Winston Churchill

World War II: Bombers

THE United States produced thousands of bombers during World War II. Among the most famous was the Boeing B-17. Called the Flying Fortress, this plane lived up to its name. It could carry over 17,000 pounds of bombs, and was armed with 12 machine guns for defense against enemy fighters. Later U.S. bombers included the Boeing B-24 Liberator and the enormous B-29 Superfortress. Many bombers were destroyed by enemy fighters and antiaircraft guns early in the war. The use of fighter escorts helped bombers complete their missions. Later bombers, such as the B-29, could fly to high altitudes beyond the reach of most enemy fire.

Bombers attacked in huge fleets of up to a thousand to knock out enemy fuel bases, arms supplies, and transportation lines. Never before had aircraft been used to destroy on such a large scale.

◀ **BOMBS AWAY!**
Flying over Burma, B-29 Superfortresses release a shower of bombs. Their target was a Japanese supply depot near Rangoon. First flown in 1944, the B-29 was the largest U.S. bomber. It could deliver a whopping 20,000 pounds of bombs.

▲ **B-24S ATTACK**
Under heavy antiaircraft fire, B-24 Liberator bombers attack an oil refinery in Romania in 1943. Black smoke rises from the ground where bombs hit the oil tanks.

▶ Flak Bait

The nose section of *Flak Bait*, a Martin B-26 Marauder bomber, is now in the National Air and Space Museum. This plane flew 200 missions over Europe, more than any other Allied bomber. Over 1,000 patches cover holes made by antiaircraft fire, or "flak."

▲ Inside Flak Bait

This interior view shows the radio and navigation station of *Flak Bait*. Visible through the door is the cockpit instrument panel. It was shattered by a German Bf 109 Messerschmitt shell in 1943. The wounded pilot managed to safely land the plane.

▶ The WASPs

Women pilots train to fly B-17 bombers at a flight school during the war. Known as the Women's Airforce Service Pilots (WASPs), they transported military aircraft to war zones. They flew everything from fighters to heavy bombers. Over 30 were killed in service.

◀ B-17 Waist Gunner

Inside a B-17 Flying Fortress, gunner Robert Taylor fires a 50-caliber machine gun to ward off attacking German fighters. He wears warm clothing and a metal-lined "flak apron" to protect against shell fire.

FUN FACT: MASS PRODUCTION

The United States was in World War II for only four years, from 1941 to 1945. Yet it produced an incredible 300,000 aircraft, including many thousand heavy bombers.

World War II: War at Sea

After Japanese warplanes bombed the U.S. naval base at Pearl Harbor in 1941, the United States entered the war. During the next years, much of the war took place at sea. From 1941 to 1945, the United States and Japan battled in the Pacific. Their most powerful weapons were aircraft carriers. Floating airfields, the huge ships known as "flattops" were 820 feet long and carried up to 100 warplanes. Fighters and bombers took off and landed on their flat decks. The carriers allowed great mobility of air attack.

In 1942, Japan launched an attack on Midway Island with four carriers. Navy dive bombers from three U.S. carriers surprised and attacked the Japanese fleet. They sank all four Japanese carriers. With the ships, Japan lost 250 planes and their most veteran pilots. This was a crippling blow that marked the turning point against Japan in the Pacific.

▲ Airship Escort

A U.S. Navy airship guards a German submarine after it has surfaced and surrendered in the Atlantic in 1945. A Navy ship waits behind. Used for coastal surveillance, airships were an important part of U.S. naval defense.

▲ KAMIKAZE

The *Cherry Blossom*, a Japanese Kugisho MXY7 Ohka kamikaze bomber, is today part of the Museum collection. Japanese kamikaze pilots flew these planes, filled with bombs, deliberately into Allied ships. They believed that suicide in such attacks was an honorable death.

◄ BULLSEYE!

U.S. Navy Douglas Dauntless dive bombers bomb the Japanese aircraft carrier *Akagi* in this painting. The bombers sank this and three other Japanese carriers near Midway Island in 1942. Most of Japan's most skilled pilots and their planes, plus 3,000 sailors, were lost.

▲ CLEARED TO GO

A signal officer aboard a U.S. carrier waves the takeoff flag for a Grumman Hellcat fighter. Carrier takeoffs and landings took great pilot skill. A net across the deck helped damaged planes returning from battle to skid safely to a stop.

Enola Gay

B y the summer of 1945, U.S. aircraft had sunk over 700,000 tons of Japanese warships and destroyed over 12,000 Japanese planes. Yet the Japanese would not surrender. Meanwhile, the United States had built the largest bomber of the war, the B-29 Superfortress. It had also secretly developed the atomic bomb.

In August, U.S. president Harry Truman decided to use the bomb to end the war and continuing loss of American lives. He ordered the flight of the B-29 *Enola Gay* to carry and drop the atomic bomb on Japan. Called "Little Boy," the weapon was a 9,700 pound uranium bomb. On August 6, 1945, the bomb was dropped over the Japanese city of Hiroshima. In seconds, the blast smashed the city and killed thousands of people. Yet Japan still did not surrender. Three days later, a 10,000 pound plutonium bomb, called "Fat Man," was dropped from a second B-29 over Nagasaki. This explosion killed thousands more. On August 15, Japan finally agreed to surrender.

▶ *Enola Gay* Cockpit

This view reveals the huge cockpit of the *Enola Gay*. Named for the pilot's mother, the B-29 had many advanced features, such as a pressurized interior and remote-controlled guns and cannon.

History Fact: Powerful Plane

The B-29 was the only bomber large and strong enough to carry heavy nuclear weapons. The B-29's power came from four supercharged 2,200-horsepower Wright engines.

▼ War Poster

A poster from the Museum collection promotes the Boeing B-29 Superfortress, first in service in 1944. The mighty bomber had a wingspan of 141 feet. A long-range craft, it could fly over 5,300 miles without refueling.

▲ MUSHROOM CLOUD
A giant cloud rises from a test explosion of an atomic bomb in the Pacific. Such blasts can generate over 100 million degrees F. of heat. Atomic bombs dropped over Hiroshima and Nagasaki wreaked terrible destruction and caused Japan's unconditional surrender.

▼ FAMOUS B-29
The *Enola Gay* comes in for a landing on its base after its historic mission. The Superfortress was donated to the National Air and Space Museum after the war.

The Sound Barrier

OWARD the end of World War II, aircraft entered a new age of speed. In 1944 and 1945, German pilots flew the first jet-powered fighter in combat, the Messerschmitt Me 262. Allied pilots were astonished to spot it zooming over 100 miles an hour faster than any Allied fighter, and with no propellers!

After the war, many pilots tried to fly faster than the speed of sound. On October 14, 1947, American test pilot Chuck Yeager flew an orange bullet-shaped plane with a rocket engine. It was the Bell X-1, designed to break the sound barrier. Carried up by a B-29 mother plane to save fuel, the X-1 was dropped in the air. Yeager fired the rocket engine and pushed the plane to over 700 miles an hour, past Mach 1—the speed of sound. The plane buffeted, then blasted through the sound barrier. Once past Mach 1, it was so smooth, said Yeager, "Grandma could be sitting up there sipping lemonade."

"Suddenly the Mach needle began to fluctuate...then tipped right off the scale. I thought I was seeing things! We were flying supersonic!"

—Chuck Yeager describing flying through the sound barrier

▲ BELL X-1
Test pilot Chuck Yeager stands beside his rocket-powered Bell X-1, named the *Glamorous Glennis* for his wife. The plane now hangs in the National Air and Space Museum. Streamlined for speed, it is shaped like a .50 caliber bullet.

▲ CHARLES "CHUCK" YEAGER (1923-   )
A World War II fighter pilot, Chuck Yeager became an Air Force test pilot after the war. He made history as the first person to break the sound barrier in 1947. At the time, many believed a plane flying through the sound barrier would be ripped apart by the shock wave. Yeager later rose to the rank of brigadier general.

▲ FAMOUS FLIGHT
On October 14, 1947, the Bell X-1 accelerates and races toward the sound barrier. Flying at 43,000 feet, pilot Chuck Yeager became the first person to travel faster than sound, at Mach 1.06.

MACHMETER

Mach numbers measure the speed of an aircraft in relation to the speed of sound. Mach 1 is the speed of sound, which increases with temperature because sound travels faster in warmer air. At 40,000 feet, Mach 1 is 657 miles an hour.

THE SOUND BARRIER

Moving through the air, a plane makes pressure waves. When the plane catches up with its own pressure waves, they bunch together, building into a shock wave. Passing the speed of sound, the plane flies ahead of its pressure waves, forming a cone-like shock wave.

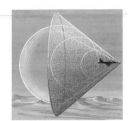

▲ FRANK WHITTLE (1907-1996)

Frank Whittle was a young British pilot who patented the first turbojet engine in 1931. It used a jet of hot gases instead of propellers. Soon after, German engineer Hans von Ohain invented a similar engine. Germany first produced a jet fighter in 1943, the Messerschmitt Me 262. A year later, the British began flying a jet fighter, the Gloster Meteor. Its engines were based on a Whittle design.

▼ MESSERSCHMITT ME 262

The first jet-propelled fighter used in combat, the German Messerschmitt Me 262 *Schwalbe* (swallow) was flown during World War II. Four 30 mm cannons made it a fearsome opponent. This Me 262 is in the Museum collection.

◄ ME 262 JET ENGINE

The Me 262 jet engine propelled the fighter to nearly 550 miles an hour. How? Air drawn into the engine front was forced into a combustion chamber, mixed with fuel, then ignited. This formed a torch-like jet of hot, burning gases. It blasted out the back of the engine with tremendous force, thrusting the plane forward.

Korea and Vietnam

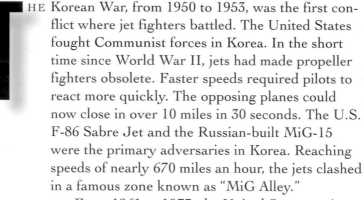

THE Korean War, from 1950 to 1953, was the first conflict where jet fighters battled. The United States fought Communist forces in Korea. In the short time since World War II, jets had made propeller fighters obsolete. Faster speeds required pilots to react more quickly. The opposing planes could now close in over 10 miles in 30 seconds. The U.S. F-86 Sabre Jet and the Russian-built MiG-15 were the primary adversaries in Korea. Reaching speeds of nearly 670 miles an hour, the jets clashed in a famous zone known as "MiG Alley."

From 1961 to 1973, the United States again fought Communist forces, this time in the Vietnam War. U.S. bombers dropped more tons of bombs in this war than both sides dropped in World War II. Helicopters played a critical role in Vietnam. Powerful helicopter gunships attacked the enemy and transported troops and supplies to the steamy jungle battle grounds. Helicopters also zoomed in to rescue wounded soldiers and downed pilots from behind enemy lines.

▲ MiG Alley
Richard Rash, an American pilot in the Korean War, walks under a sign for "MiG Alley" in Korea in 1952. Mig Alley was a combat zone over the Yalu River valley along North Korea's northern border, where U.S. jets battled Russian MiGs.

◄ F-86 Sabre Jet
Streaking through the sky, a North American F-86 Sabre Jet fires rockets at a target. The first U.S. jet with swept-back wings, the Sabre Jet dominated battles in Korea. Flown by U.S. pilots, it won over its MiG-15 opponent at a rate of 10 to 1.

▲ Checking It Out
Mechanics in Okinawa check a captured MiG-15 repainted with U.S. Air Force markings in 1953. Test pilots who flew this MiG said that overall, the F-86 was a better plane.

◄ MiG-15s

Three MiG-15s race in formation over Korea. Quick and agile, the MiG could climb and fly faster than the F-86. Yet its Communist Chinese and Korean pilots were less skilled than the World War II veteran U.S. pilots.

► Eject!
With jets' faster speed, pilots no longer bailed out. This Navy pilot springs from his plane in an ejection seat. A parachute will open to land him safely on the ground.

⊳⊳ To the Rescue

The interior of the Sikorsky HH-3E helicopter (right) was a welcome sight to many U.S. fighter pilots in Vietnam. Armed with heavy guns, the chopper flew in to rescue pilots downed in battle. It flew wounded men to base hospitals.

◂ Green Giant

Painted in olive green camouflage, the Sikorsky HH-3E was a large, powerful helicopter affectionately called the "Jolly Green Giant." A beacon of hope for stranded soldiers as well as pilots, it saved many lives in the war.

▲ McDonnell F-4 Phantom II

Flying night reconnaissance, an F-4 Phantom II fighter crosses Vietnam in this painting. Able to race twice the speed of sound, the F-4 was a versatile plane. The first jet to find and destroy targets by radar without ground support, it excelled in dogfights with MiG-21 jets and also served as a bomber.

⊳ Republic F-105D Thunderchief

Laden with bombs, two F-105D Thunderchief fighter-bombers head toward targets. The F-105D could carry over 12,000 pounds of bombs. It flew a large number of air strikes in Vietnam. As a fighter, it could deliver an amazing six thousand rounds of cannon fire per minute.

Modern Military Aircraft

WARS over the last decades have greatly changed and advanced military aircraft. The development of more sophisticated technology in radar, navigation, and weapons systems has produced faster, stronger, and more complex jet fighters and bombers.

Aircraft carriers have also changed. Jets are heavier than propeller aircraft. They require the boost of a catapult, like a giant slingshot, to launch them from the carrier deck. Carriers now have a catapult officer in charge of launching, called a "shooter." In a launch, a catapult hurls the plane from a standstill to a speed of 200 miles an hour in the air. Strong arresting cables on deck help the jets land safely. The jets have a tailhook to snag the cables as they land.

Modern carriers, up to 1,100 feet long, are like floating air bases. They may carry nearly 100 planes. These carrier-based aircraft have been active in conflicts and peacekeeping from Vietnam to the present.

▲ Bombers

Today's bombers include both old and new. The B-1B (above) is a modern long-range bomber with advanced radar for precision bombing. Its swing-wing design can change the wings from forward takeoff position to swept-back position for high-speed attack. The B-52 bomber (below) has flown since 1952. Armed with missiles, it served in the Persian Gulf War.

◄ Air Base at Sea

Jet fighters fly in formation over the carrier USS *John C. Stennis*. The big ship bristles with aircraft, including F-14 Tomcat and F-18 Hornet fighters, S 3B Vikings, EA-6B Prowlers, and E-2C Hawkeye AWACS surveillance planes.

▼ Military Jets

An AV-88 Harrier "jump jet" (top) lifts straight up in a vertical takeoff. Its jet nozzles can be directed to take off, hover, or land like a helicopter or fly straight ahead. F-18 Hornet fighters (center) line an aircraft carrier deck. Bottom, a Hornet launches from the deck.

Modern Fighters

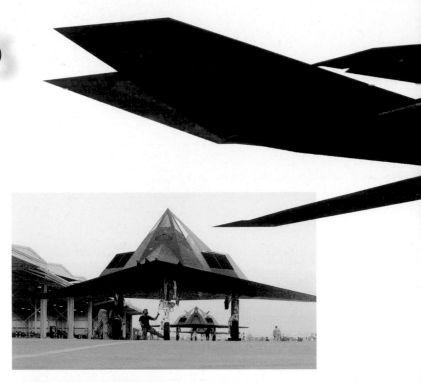

ODAY'S jet fighters are among the fastest planes ever built. The F-16 Fighting Falcon, for example, can fly at more than twice the speed of sound. Modern fighters use "fly by wire" flight. This means physical cables no longer pull on control surfaces such as the rudder. Instead, computers send signals along electric wires to motors that move control surfaces.

To increase speed, supersonic fighters today have streamlined bodies with pointed noses and swept-back or arrow-shaped wings. Some have ultra-thin wing edges to reduce drag and cut through air easily at high speeds. To withstand the scorching heat of supersonic speeds, the planes have "skins" of heat-resistant metals such as titanium.

Most fighters intercept and attack other aircraft. They may also attack ground targets. Pilots today locate targets electronically and fire deadly radar-guided or heat-seeking missiles. Modern fighters can cost up to $30 million each! Much of the cost is for electronic radar, flight, and navigation systems.

▲ F-16 Fighting Falcon

Two F-16 Falcons zoom over canyons in Utah on a training mission. Fast and highly maneuverable, the F-16 excels at air combat or ground attack. Armed with cannon and missiles, it can fly up to 1,345 miles an hour.

▶ F-18 Hornet Research Fighter

This F-18 has been modified to test a new feature. Strakes, hinged structures on its nose, open to stabilize the jet as it dives at a steep angle of attack. They give the pilot better handling in an otherwise dangerous maneuver.

▲ LOCKHEED F-117A NIGHTHAWK

The first "stealth" plane in combat, the F-117A (above and left) flew in the Persian Gulf War in 1991. Its shape and special paint scatter radar beams to help it fly undetected. Hunting at night, the Nighthawk fires laser-guided missiles.

➤ THUNDERBIRDS ON DISPLAY

F-16 Thunderbirds, the U.S. Air Force demonstration team, roar into a Diamond formation. A pilot's view (below) shows how close the jets fly. Such maneuvers showcase both the pilots' precision and skill and the capabilities of the F-16.

◄ A-10 THUNDERBOLT II

Sweeping down from the sky, an A-10 Thunderbolt II dives to attack. Designed to support ground troops, it can fly low and slow to destroy targets such as tanks with guns and missiles. The A-10 served in rescue missions during the Gulf War.

Spy in the Sky

FOR years a top secret, the existence of military spy planes made world headlines in 1960 when one was captured. Francis Gary Powers, American pilot of a U-2 reconnaissance jet, was caught spying over the Soviet Union and shot down.

The U-2 was designed in the 1950s, during the Cold War between the United States and Soviet Union. It was a long-winged, glider-like plane with a panoramic camera. Flying at high altitudes, it took photographs to search for Soviet ballistic missiles.

In the 1960s, another spy plane, the Lockheed SR-71 Blackbird, was introduced. It could fly even higher and faster than the U-2 and photograph 100,000 square miles. The first stealth plane, it had a flattened shape and dark coating that helped it elude radar.

Today, spy planes fly missions to monitor world hot spots. By giving warning of dangerous conflicts, they help world leaders plan strategies.

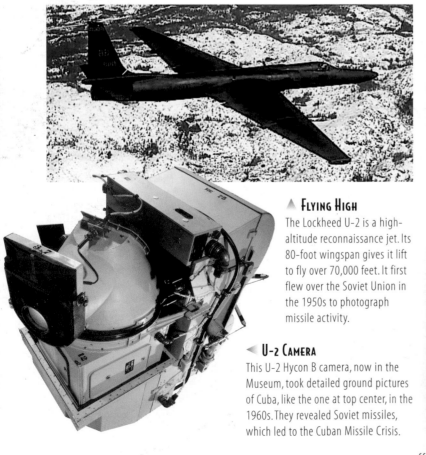

▲ Flying High
The Lockheed U-2 is a high-altitude reconnaissance jet. Its 80-foot wingspan gives it lift to fly over 70,000 feet. It first flew over the Soviet Union in the 1950s to photograph missile activity.

◄ U-2 Camera
This U-2 Hycon B camera, now in the Museum, took detailed ground pictures of Cuba, like the one at top center, in the 1960s. They revealed Soviet missiles, which led to the Cuban Missile Crisis.

Pilot's Seat

A maze of dials and controls surrounds the pilot in the SR-71 cockpit. When the craft rips through the sky at full speed, the windscreen gets so hot pilots cannot touch it long, even with heavy gloves. Some pilots use the screen to heat food!

Lockheed SR-71

This high-altitude spy plane flew faster than any other aircraft. It set a speed record of 2,193 miles an hour. Like the U-2, it took reconnaissance photographs. The plane's shape and dark color earned it the name "Blackbird."

B-2 Stealth Bomber

One of the most technically advanced of all aircraft, the B-2 Stealth Bomber has a flying wing design and sophisticated computer technology. Its shape and dark coating help it penetrate enemy defenses without detection. First test flown in 1989, it served in the Balkans and Iraq.

Global Hawk

This experimental unmanned aircraft was developed by the Air Force. Its mission is to give military commanders a high-altitude, long-endurance system to photograph large geographic areas.

FUN FACT: SPEEDY SPY PLANE

The SR-71 could fly at altitudes of 90,000 feet and as fast as Mach 3.3. It set several speed records, including a flight between Los Angeles, California and Washington, D.C. in just 64 minutes!

Jet Transport

J ET power, first used in World War II, transformed the world of flight. With superior thrust, jet engines allowed planes to fly longer distances at higher speeds. In 1952, the first commercial jetliner, the British De Havilland Comet, began service.

The Comet flew 490 miles an hour, faster than any other passenger plane. Its 44 passengers traveled eight miles up in a comfortable pressurized cabin. Quiet jet engines made the ride smooth and relaxing. Yet in 1954, two Comets exploded in midair. The cause was high-altitude stress on the plane's metal body.

The next jet airliners were built with strong, pressure-resistant fuselages. The American Boeing 707, introduced in 1957, was safe, fast, and comfortable, with 143 seats. In 1969, Boeing built the first jumbo jet—the 747. This became the world's most successful jetliner. With a wide-body fuselage that can seat over 400, it lowered the cost of air travel. Today, millions of people around the world have flown in the 747.

◄ AIR TRAFFIC CONTROL

In the control tower at an airport, air traffic controllers track aircraft on radar screens. Each symbol on the screen indicates a plane's position in its flight path. Controllers communicate with pilots by radio to safely guide each plane.

► DOUBLE-DECKER

At 239 feet long and weighing 1.2 million pounds, Europe's new Airbus 380 is the world's largest passenger airliner. It has a second deck that runs the length of the aircraft, allowing it to carry up to 853 passengers.

◀ Boeing 707

Sleek and streamlined, the Boeing 707 was the first U.S. jet transport airliner. It measured 144 feet long, with a wingspan of 130 feet. Flying nearly 600 miles an hour, it cut previous travel time nearly in half.

▼ The President's Plane

Air Force One, a Boeing 747, soars majestically over Mount Rushmore, South Dakota. This plane carries the President of the United States on business around the world. It has a special interior for the President.

▲ Concorde

The Concorde, developed by the British and French, is the world's only supersonic jetliner. It first flew in 1969. Able to fly over twice the speed of sound, it could whisk passengers across the Atlantic in three and a half hours. The crash of an Air France Concorde in 2000 resulted in the grounding of all Concordes for safety testing.

▼ With Our Compliments

Many jet airlines offered passengers convenient overnight kits. This collection from the Museum includes an array of kit bags with items such as combs, pens, airsick bags, toothbrushes, and a sleeping mask.

FUN FACT: MODERN AIRPORTS

Today over one billion people a year use U.S. airports. Air traffic controllers in the United States monitor more than 200,000 takeoffs and landings each day.

FUN FACT: SUM OF MANY PARTS

The Boeing 747 is made up of about $4\frac{1}{2}$ million parts made in many different countries.

Helicopters

UNLIKE fixed-wing airplanes, helicopters have whirling rotary wings, called rotors. Helicopters can fly forwards, backwards, sideways, straight up or down, and hover in one spot. The idea of the helicopter is very old. The ancient Chinese had a toy helicopter, called a "flying top." Early designers, including Sir George Cayley, inventor of the glider, envisioned helicopters. Yet it was not until much later that real helicopters appeared. In 1907, Frenchman Paul Cornu built and flew a helicopter in the first free flight. The double-rotor craft rose five feet off the ground for 20 seconds.

The first practical single-rotor helicopters were invented by Igor Sikorsky in the 1930s. Since then, helicopters have performed many tasks other planes cannot. Because they can take off and land in small spaces and hover, helicopters serve as rescue craft, flying ambulances, lifting vehicles, and traffic observers. Modern helicopters range from small, light craft to heavy military gunships and transports.

◀ IGOR SIKORSKY (1889-1972)
Russian-born inventor Igor Sikorsky, known as the father of the modern helicopter, began work on helicopters in 1909. At the time, engines were too heavy to be practical for these craft. Sikorsky designed many other aircraft. Then in the 1930s, he returned to helicopters. At left, he test pilots his single-rotor VS-300 on its first flight in 1939. Sikorsky went on to design several successful helicopters, including a huge craft that could lift 18 tons of cargo.

▲ PRESIDENT'S HELICOPTER
In 1957, this Bell 47J helicopter was bought for use by President Dwight D. Eisenhower. Ever since, presidents have used helicopters for short trips between the White House and nearby posts, such as Camp David. This presidential craft was presented to the National Air and Space Museum in 1967.

FUN FACT: NAME GAME
The word "helicopter" comes from the Greek words for "spiral" and "wing." Helicopters have had many nicknames, including "chopper," "whirly bird," "eggbeater," and "handy andy."

▶ TROOP TRANSPORTER
Flying over the thick jungles of Vietnam, a Bell UH-1 Huey military helicopter ferries soldiers to a battle area. The men can jump quickly out of the doors into cover on landing. Thousands of helicopters, including gunships, transporters, and rescue craft, served in Vietnam.

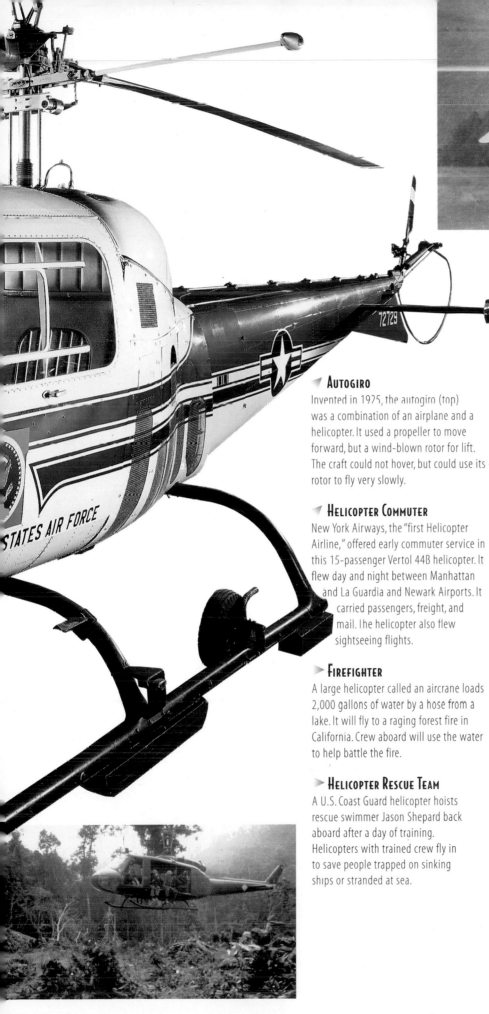

Autogiro

Invented in 1925, the autogiro (top) was a combination of an airplane and a helicopter. It used a propeller to move forward, but a wind-blown rotor for lift. The craft could not hover, but could use its rotor to fly very slowly.

Helicopter Commuter

New York Airways, the "first Helicopter Airline," offered early commuter service in this 15-passenger Vertol 44B helicopter. It flew day and night between Manhattan and La Guardia and Newark Airports. It carried passengers, freight, and mail. The helicopter also flew sightseeing flights.

Firefighter

A large helicopter called an aircrane loads 2,000 gallons of water by a hose from a lake. It will fly to a raging forest fire in California. Crew aboard will use the water to help battle the fire.

Helicopter Rescue Team

A U.S. Coast Guard helicopter hoists rescue swimmer Jason Shepard back aboard after a day of training. Helicopters with trained crew fly in to save people trapped on sinking ships or stranded at sea.

Working Planes

ODAY, specialized aircraft perform a variety of important jobs. Planes transport military troops, carry relief cargoes of food and medicine to people in disaster-hit areas, dust crops with chemicals to fight insect pests, fight fires, patrol large areas, and monitor weather conditions. In remote or wilderness regions, rugged bush planes are the only way doctors and other people can reach isolated outposts. In war zones, large transport aircraft move and drop thousands of military troops.

Some planes are small craft designed for fun, sport, and leisure flying. Each year, inventors continue to design innovative new aircraft to perform even more jobs.

▲ Piper Cub
A flying classic, the Piper Cub J-3 was introduced in 1936. This two-seat light plane is now in the Museum. Cubs were used as trainers for military and private pilots and flown for recreation. The Cub's cruising speed was 80 miles an hour.

▲ Weather Aircraft
A Weather Service DC-6 (top) has a long gust probe and other instruments to gather weather data aloft. This helps forecasters predict weather systems. Above, visitors inspect an Orion P-3 hurricane hunter plane. It flies into the huge whirling storms to pinpoint their position and strength for hurricane forecasters in Miami. Symbols on the plane's side indicate hurricanes the plane has tracked.

Bush Plane

A hunter poses with his game and a Noorduyn Norseman float plane he flew on a hunting trip in Canada. Bush planes carry hunters, wilderness explorers, and medical teams to remote spots no other transportation can reach.

It's a Car, It's a Plane

Called the "Flying Car," a 1947 Convair Model 118 ConAirCar consisted of a two-seater car and an aircraft frame with a 180 horsepower engine. Designed for convenient personal use, it was meant to fly and drive. Unfortunately, it ran out of gas in flight and crashed.

Parachute Drop

Military paratroopers jump from a C-141B Starlifter during a training mission. The Starlifter transports combat troops over long distances. It delivers both soldiers and supplies and also carries wounded soldiers to hospitals.

Water Bomber

Whoosh! A C-130 Hercules drops a load of water mixed with fire retardant chemicals over a forest fire in California. The versatile C-130 is also widely used as a military transport and cargo plane.

Airlift

Members of the 82nd Airborne Division wait to be airlifted by transport planes at Fort Bragg, North Carolina. Military planes can move many thousands of forces quickly to training stations or combat zones.

Modern Record Breakers

N the last few decades, aviators have continued to set new records. In 1977, American cyclist Bryan Allen used leg muscle to pedal the first human-powered aircraft, the *Gossamer Condor*. A pedaling mechanism drove a propeller, powering the craft to 11 miles an hour. Made of cardboard, aluminum, and plastic, the ultra-light plane weighed 207 pounds, including the pilot! In 1980, Allen pedaled *Gossamer Albatross* over the English Channel.

In 1986, pilots Dick Rutan and Jeana Yeager set a milestone aviation record, flying nonstop around the world without refueling. They made the trip in nine days in the *Voyager*. Extra fuel tanks were built in the plane's long, thin wings.

Finally in 1999, the *Breitling Orbiter 3*, a shiny silver-colored balloon, made the first round-the-world balloon trip. Swiss pilot Bertrand Piccard and British co-pilot Brian Jones flew for 30,000 miles, crossing mountains, deserts, and the Pacific and Atlantic Oceans.

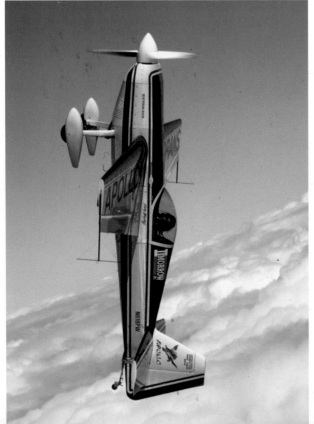

◀ AEROBATIC EXTRA 260
Climbing straight up, aerobatic pilot Patty Wagstaff performs precision turns, rolls, dives, and other maneuvers in her Extra 260. Wagstaff won the U.S. National Aerobatic Championships in 1991, 92, and 93 in this plane, now on display in the National Air and Space Museum.

▲ RUTAN VOYAGER
Built of light graphite fiber with a wingspan of 111 feet, the Rutan *Voyager* soars on its round-the-world flight in 1986. The plane carried 1,200 gallons of fuel. Today, the *Voyager* hangs in the Museum.

GOSSAMER ALBATROSS

In 1980, cyclist Bryan Allen test-flies the *Gossamer Albatross*, a human-powered craft operated by pedaling. Flown by Allen, the *Gossamer Albatross* won the Kremer Prize for human-powered flight when it crossed the English Channel.

BREITLING ORBITER 3

Covered with a skin of silver mylar, the *Breitling Orbiter 3* was filled with helium and hot air. The balloon's gondola (below) held tanks of propane fuel, oxygen to breathe, and tiny crew quarters. It is today displayed in the Museum.

"For us it was...very emotional — to feel the luck we had to fly around this beautiful world."

—Bertrand Piccard, co-pilot of the *Breitling Orbiter 3*

AROUND THE WORLD IN 20 DAYS

Breitling Orbiter 3 drifts over the Alps on its 30,000-mile journey around the globe in 1999. The long trip also set a balloon flight duration record of 19 days, 21 hours, and 55 minutes.

Rockets and the Space Age

ROCKETS have been around for centuries. The Chinese used gunpowder rockets as weapons as early as the 13th century. They filled pointed bamboo tubes with gunpowder, sealed one end and lit the other. The explosion created a thrust, or pushing force, that propelled the rocket the opposite way. Rockets were later fired in the War of 1812. Francis Scott Key described their "red glare" in the "Star Spangled Banner."

In the 20th century, scientists developed rockets to explore space. Rocket engines are the only engines that can operate in the vacuum of space. In space there is no air, and so no oxygen. Rockets carry both fuel and their own oxygen supply, called an oxidizer. Large rockets can also produce tremendous power, enough to escape Earth's gravity. In 1926, American scientist Dr. Robert Goddard launched the first liquid-propellant rocket. He concluded that a rocket could be more efficiently propelled by liquid fuel. In World War II, Germany built powerful rocket weapons. Then in 1957, the Soviet Union stunned the world by using a rocket to launch the first Earth-orbiting satellite, Sputnik.

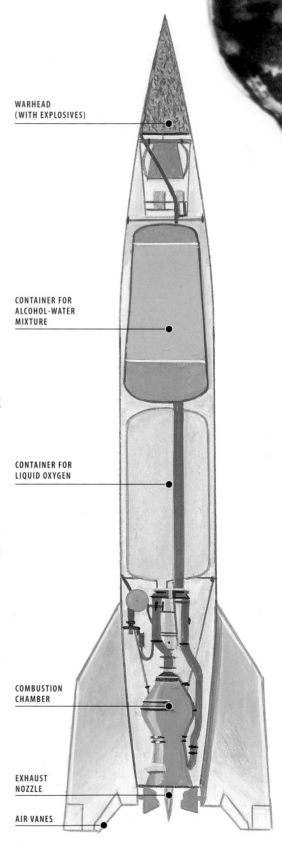

WARHEAD
(WITH EXPLOSIVES)

CONTAINER FOR
ALCOHOL-WATER
MIXTURE

CONTAINER FOR
LIQUID OXYGEN

COMBUSTION
CHAMBER

EXHAUST
NOZZLE

AIR VANES

◀ ◀ V-2 "Vengeance Weapon"
One of Germany's most frightening weapons, a V-2 rocket roars into the sky during World War II. The first long-range ballistic missile, it carried 2,000 pounds of explosives. Over 3,000 were fired at Britain and other targets.

◀ Ready for Launch
Germans prepare a V-2 for launching. Small by modern standards, the V-2 was 46 feet tall. The forerunner of later rockets, it could race 150 miles in five minutes and destroy whole city blocks.

▶ Inside the V-2
The V-2 got its powerful thrust by burning alcohol using liquid oxygen. These were mixed and ignited in a combustion chamber, creating hot gases. As they expanded they burst from the rocket's nozzle, forcing it upward. The V-2's explosives were carried in its nose.

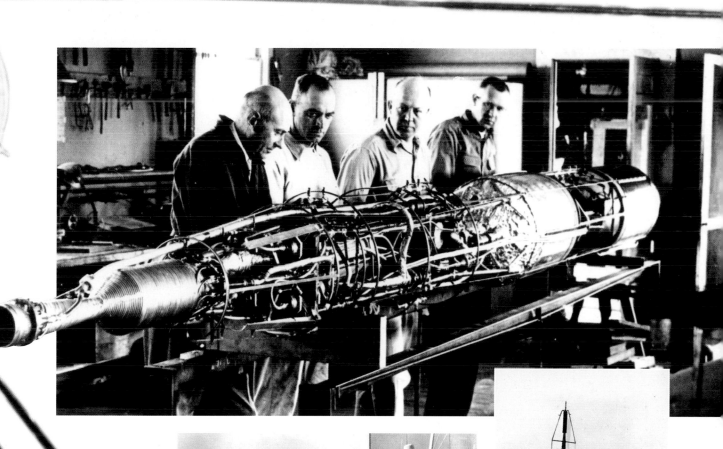

▲ Sputnik

On October 4, 1957, a Soviet rocket launched the first satellite, Sputnik ("Traveling Companion"). A metal ball 23 inches across, it orbited Earth, sending "beep, beep" radio signals. A replica of Sputnik hangs in the Museum.

▼ R-7 Rocket

The 100-foot-high Soviet R-7 rocket which launched Sputnik was the biggest rocket in existence at the time. At liftoff, its five powerful rocket engines generated about 900,000 pounds of thrust, 16 times as much as the V-2.

▲ ▲ Goddard 1941 Rocket

In 1941, Dr. Robert Goddard (top picture, left) examines one of his most advanced rockets as his assistants watch. This 22-foot-high test rocket was fueled with gasoline and liquid oxygen. It is today displayed in the National Air and Space Museum.

▲ 1935 A-3 Rocket

Three of Dr. Goddard's assistants lift his liquid-fueled A-3 rocket to fit it into a launch tower in Roswell, New Mexico. In the secluded southwest desert, Goddard tested many of his inventions.

▲ Robert H. Goddard (1882-1945)

Dr. Robert H. Goddard, inventor of the first flying liquid-propellant rocket, stands beside his creation. On March 16, 1926, the Massachusetts physics professor launched the rocket from his aunt's farm in Auburn, Massachusetts. Fueled with liquid oxygen and gasoline, it shot up 41 feet in 2½ seconds. Goddard envisioned multi-stage rockets and using rockets to reach the Moon. He is considered the father of American rocketry.

To the Edge of Space

THE space age began with the launch of Sputnik in 1957. In 1959, the United States began testing a new aircraft. Sleek, streamlined, and rocket-powered, the North American X-15 was the fastest, highest-flying airplane ever built. Its purpose was to fly to the end of the atmosphere and up into the edge of space. It gathered information that was later of great use to engineers planning a U.S. space program.

The X-15 was made of a strong heat-resistant metal alloy to endure the heat of hypersonic (many times faster than sound) speeds. It was able to withstand 1,300 degrees Fahrenheit. The X-15 flew to an incredible 354,200 feet, over 67 miles high, and reached a speed of 4,520 miles an hour, or Mach 6.7. The pilot used air controls in the atmosphere and fired rocket thrusters to maneuver in space. How did he know which controls to use? Test pilot Scott Crossfield said, "When one didn't work, I simply used the other."

▲ Mother Ship
A huge B-52 bomber carries the X-15 under its wing to take it up to launching altitude. At 38,000 feet, the B-52 released the X-15, which fired its powerful rocket engine and took off.

▲ M2-F1 in Flight
A pilot brings the M2-F1 lifting body in to land on a dry lake bed after a test flight in 1962. Data gathered in tests of lifting bodies was later used to design the space shuttle.

➤ M2-F3 Lifting Body
Another experimental vehicle was a wingless aircraft called a "lifting body." Launched in mid-air from a B-52, the craft could fly about 17 miles high at nearly 1,240 miles an hour. This Northrop M2-F3 now hangs in the Museum.

◄ ASTRONAUT WINGS

Five pilots who flew the X-15 went so high they were awarded astronaut wings for space travel. Space is considered to begin at an altitude of 50 miles. The X-15 flew to over 67 miles.

➤ NORTH AMERICAN X-15

In 1967, this rocket-powered research plane reached the threshold of space. It flew to 354,200 feet, a record for winged craft that still stands. One of the three X-15s built now hangs in the National Air and Space Museum.

◄ SKY SIGNATURE

Rocketing toward the Sun, the X-15 leaves a long plume of condensed vapor, a contrail, in the sky. Back on the ground (above), the X-15 gets a checkup as its B-52 mother plane flies overhead. The X-15 was the first plane to fly past Mach 6.

FUN FACT: FAST TRIP

The X-15's top speed of 4,520 miles an hour is fast enough to zip across the United States from coast to coast in 40 minutes!

Mercury and Gemini

B Y the 1960s, the United States was competing with the Soviet Union for supremacy in a "Space Race." Both nations launched rockets carrying animals—dogs and monkeys—to test space flight on living things.

On April 12, 1961, the Soviet Union moved ahead in the race by putting the first man into orbit. He was cosmonaut, or "sailor of the cosmos," Yuri Gagarin. The United States responded with its piloted Mercury spacecraft. The first one, on May 5, 1961, carried astronaut, or "star sailor," Alan Shepard on a 15-minute flight that did not go into orbit. On February 20, 1962, Mercury's *Friendship 7* blasted into orbit with John Glenn.

The next step was Gemini, a two-person spacecraft program. Gemini astronauts practiced docking with other spacecraft and other skills that would be needed for a mission to the Moon. Now the race to the Moon was on!

▲ Alan Shepard (1923-1998)

Alan Shepard was the first American in space. A month after Yuri Gagarin of the Soviet Union orbited the Earth, Shepard was launched 117 miles into space in the Mercury *Freedom 7* capsule (above). He made a suborbital flight and returned to Earth 15 minutes later. Unlike Gagarin, Shepard had some manual control of his craft. Shepard later explored the Moon on an Apollo mission.

◀ Mercury Seven

America's first astronauts, and big heroes at home, pose for a group portrait in 1962. From left: Wally Schirra, Alan Shepard, Deke Slayton, Gus Grissom, John Glenn, Gordon Cooper, and Scott Carpenter.

▶ Mercury and Gemini Capsules

This painting compares the sizes of the first U.S. spacecraft. The smaller Mercury capsule carried one astronaut. The Gemini capsule carried two. Visitors to the Museum can see both the Mercury *Friendship 7* and the Gemini 4.

FUN FACT: NAME THAT SHIP

Each astronaut named the capsule he flew in during Mercury. Alan Shepard named his capsule *Freedom* and John Glenn named his *Friendship*. Later ships were called *Liberty Bell*, *Aurora*, *Sigma*, and *Faith*.

⬧ GEMINI FIRSTS

A hundred miles above the Earth, Gemini 4 astronaut Ed White takes the first U.S. spacewalk June 3, 1965. It lasted 23 minutes. On December 15, 1965, Gemini 6 edges to within a few feet of Gemini 7 in the first rendezvous of piloted U.S. spacecraft.

▼ SNUG FIT

Inside the tiny cabin of *Freedom 7*, Mercury astronaut Alan Shepard lies in a couch surrounded by instruments. The first U.S. piloted spacecraft, it was just big enough for one person to squeeze into.

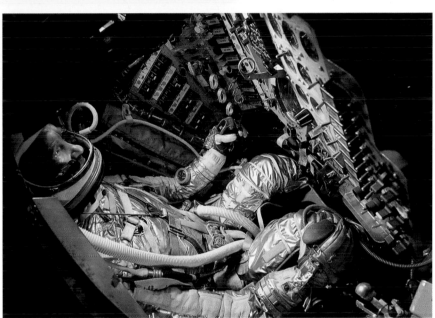

➤ JOHN GLENN (1921 –   )

On February 20, 1962, John Glenn (right) became the first American to orbit the Earth. He was shot into space in the Mercury *Friendship 7*, and circled the Earth three times. When the spacecraft's automatic controls malfunctioned, Glenn manually flew the ship and kept it on course. He was the first person to do so. Glenn kept flight notes in the notebook at right. After his career as an astronaut, Glenn served as a U.S. senator from Ohio. In 1998, he again flew in space aboard the space shuttle.

Comparative Rockets

"**T**HREE, two, one—we have liftoff!" With these words, rocket engines explode with a deafening roar, spewing out columns of fire and gas. Smoke billows into the sky and the ground shakes as the mighty engines thrust the rocket into the sky and send it hurtling toward space.

On these pages you can see rockets of many sizes and shapes developed during the Space Age. They were built for many purposes. Some were used as missiles, or weapons. Others were used as launching vehicles to send communications or weather satellites into space. And some have launched spacecraft with animals and human beings into space.

The Saturn V rockets were the largest, most powerful ever built. They were used to launch the Apollo missions to the Moon. Each Saturn V rocket had three stages. Stacked all together, the rocket stood nearly as tall as a 40 story building! It weighed over 3,000 tons, most of that nearly 2,950 tons of rocket fuel.

◄ Apollo 11 Launch
Seconds after ignition, Apollo 11 rises as a tower of flames pours from Saturn V's engines. In 2½ minutes, the first stage boosted the craft 35 miles above Earth, traveling 6,000 miles an hour. Then the second stage fired.

▼ First to Fly
The Russian cosmonaut Yuri Gagarin, seen here on a magazine cover with Soviet leader Nikita Khrushchev, was the first human to fly in space, in Vostok 1. His successful flight touched off the U.S.-U.S.S.R. race to the Moon.

▲ Stage One
The first stage of Saturn V was 138 feet long. Its five massive engines, here covered, generated 7.6 million pounds of thrust. Each one used 5,000 gallons of fuel a second.

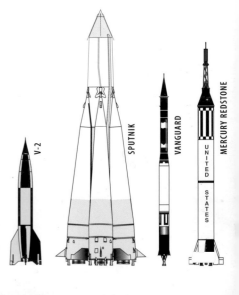

V-2

SPUTNIK

VANGUARD

MERCURY REDSTONE

▶ SPACE SHUTTLE

Trailing clouds of steam and fire, the space shuttle *Endeavour* thunders into the sky. The shuttle's twin rocket boosters along with its main engines lift the ship up toward Earth orbit.

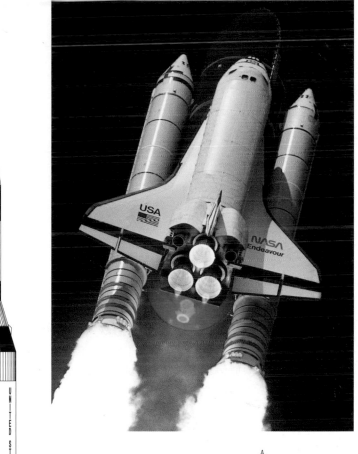

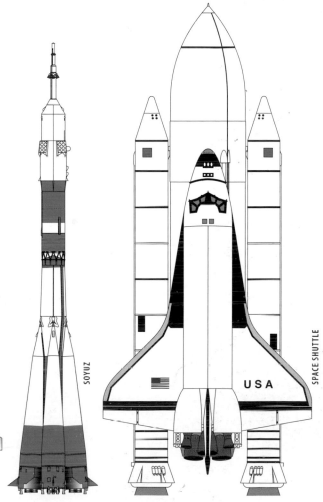

MERCURY ATLAS

GEMINI TITAN II

VOSTOK

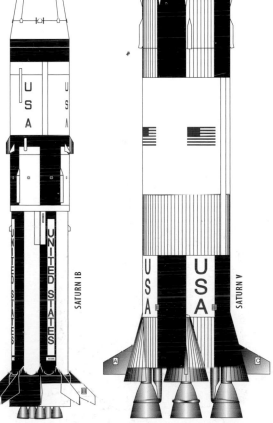

SATURN IB

SATURN V

SOYUZ

SPACE SHUTTLE

Apollo to the Moon

IN 1961, President John F. Kennedy declared that America would land a man on the Moon and bring him back safely by the end of the decade. On July 16, 1969, the first craft scheduled for a Moon landing, Apollo 11, lifted off. On the craft were astronauts Neil Armstrong, Michael Collins, and Buzz Aldrin.

The spacecraft had three parts: The command module carried the astronauts to and from the Moon. The size of a large automobile, it was where the astronauts ate, slept, and worked. The service module contained fuel and power equipment. The combined command and service module unit was called *Columbia*. The lunar module, called the *Eagle*, was the vehicle to land two astronauts on the Moon.

After breaking away from earth's gravity, Apollo 11 set a course for the Moon. Michael Collins separated *Columbia* from the *Eagle*, then maneuvered around to dock with *Eagle* in position for the Moon landing. It took three days of traveling to reach the Moon. An amazing event in history was about to happen.

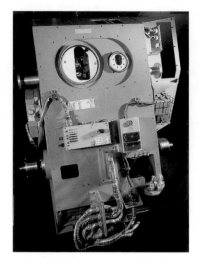

▲ ONBOARD COMPUTER

This computer, in the Museum's collection, controlled many systems on the Apollo 11 spacecraft, including its movements in space. Sometimes the astronauts switched to manual controls to steer the craft if they saw unexpected obstacles in the way.

▶ READY FOR LAUNCH

In this scene, experts gather at an early launch control center at Cape Canaveral, Florida, for the launch of an early Saturn rocket. Some peer up periscopes to check the rocket. Today, a control center at Kennedy Space Center in Florida monitors launches. After liftoff, Mission Control in Houston, Texas, takes over monitoring the spacecraft.

◀ LOG BOOK

Apollo 11 astronauts took this log book along on their historic mission to the Moon. It gives instructions for tasks they performed in flight, including photographing clouds and other objects for scientists on Earth to study.

FUN FACT: SPACE MEALS

Talk about fast food! The Apollo 11 astronauts ate freeze-dried meals that were lightweight and easily stored in sealed packets. A typical meal? Dried chicken and rice, biscuit cubes, and juice. The astronauts squirted water into the bags of dry foods to eat them.

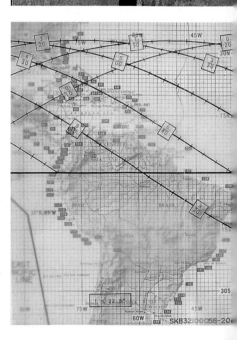

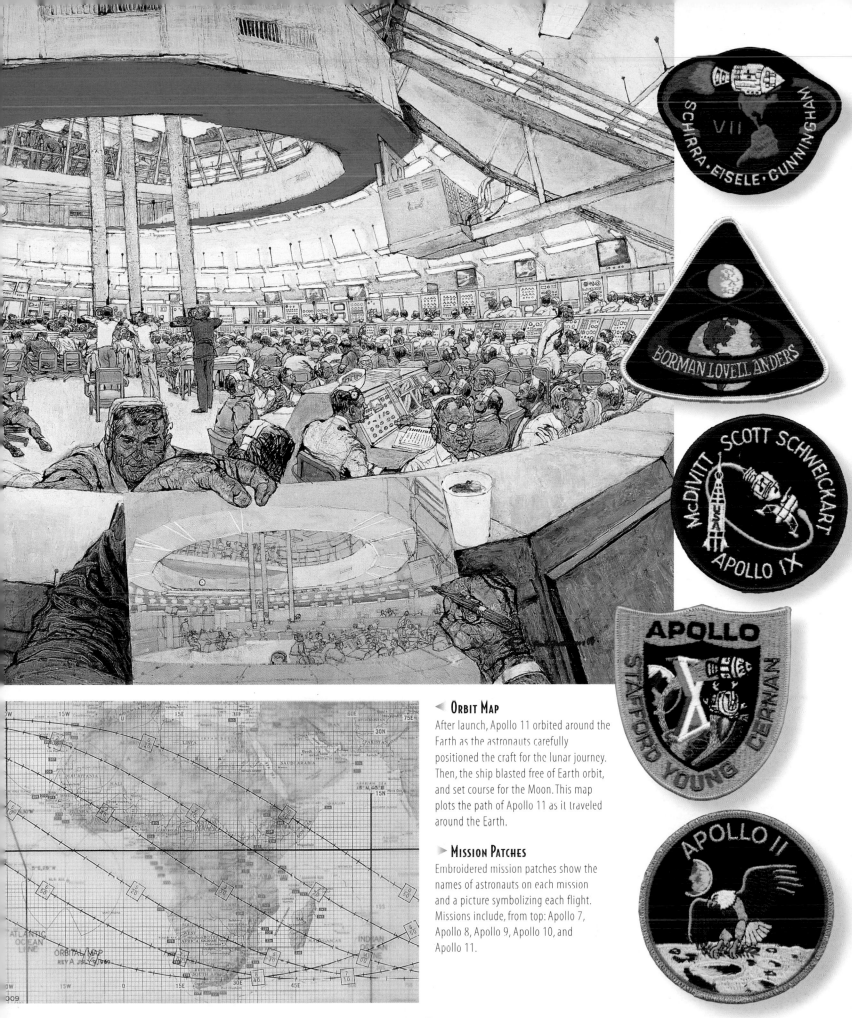

◄ Orbit Map

After launch, Apollo 11 orbited around the Earth as the astronauts carefully positioned the craft for the lunar journey. Then, the ship blasted free of Earth orbit, and set course for the Moon. This map plots the path of Apollo 11 as it traveled around the Earth.

► Mission Patches

Embroidered mission patches show the names of astronauts on each mission and a picture symbolizing each flight. Missions include, from top: Apollo 7, Apollo 8, Apollo 9, Apollo 10, and Apollo 11.

One Small Step

O N July 19, 1969, Apollo 11 reached lunar orbit. The next day Michael Collins piloted *Columbia* in orbit around the Moon as the other two astronauts crawled into the lunar module *Eagle*. Neil Armstrong fired *Eagle*'s descent engine. Then he gently landed *Eagle*'s spiderlike legs on the Moon's surface. In words broadcast to Earth, he announced to Mission Control in Houston, Texas: "The *Eagle* has landed."

Dressed in a space suit, Armstrong opened *Eagle*'s hatch and stepped down onto the Moon. The first human to explore a new world, he described his step as a "giant leap for mankind." Buzz Aldrin soon followed. A TV camera showed the amazing event to viewers on Earth. The two astronauts spent 2 hours on the Moon's surface. They planted an American flag, collected Moon rocks, took photographs and scientific measurements, and received a telephone call from President Richard Nixon. Finally, they returned to the *Eagle*. After 21 hours and 36 minutes on the Moon, they lifted off to dock with *Columbia* for the journey home.

"That's one small step for man, one giant leap for mankind."

—Neil Armstrong, first man to step on the Moon
July 20, 1969

◀ Greetings From Earth

During their historic visit to the Moon, Apollo 11 astronauts left this aluminum plaque behind. Its message of peace was signed by all three astronauts and by U.S. President Richard M. Nixon.

▶ Moon Visitor

The second man on the Moon, astronaut Buzz Aldrin climbs down the ladder of the lunar module *Eagle* to the lunar surface. He and astronaut Neil Armstrong explored the Moon's surface and collected lunar rock and soil samples.

FUN FACT: NEW MINERAL

The astronauts collected many rocks and found new Moon minerals. One was named "armalcolite," combining names of the three Apollo 11 astronauts.

FUN FACT: FEELING LIGHT

The Moon's gravity is one-sixth that of Earth's. This allowed the astronauts on the Moon to jump high easily. If you jumped lightly on the Moon, it would feel like bouncing on a trampoline.

▲ Apollo 11 Crew

Astronauts of Apollo 11 made the first successful landing on the Moon. From left: Neil Armstrong, flight commander, Michael Collins, pilot of the command module *Columbia*, and Edwin "Buzz" Aldrin, Jr., co-pilot of the lunar module *Eagle*.

▼ Splashdown

After reentering Earth's atmosphere, protected from the fiery heat by their spacecraft's heat shield, the astronauts splashed down in the Pacific Ocean. Navy divers arrived by helicopter to rescue them.

▶ Welcome Home!

In New York City, the Apollo 11 crew gets a hero's welcome. The crew was honored by crowds of cheering fans in one of the biggest ticker-tape parades in the city's history.

Exploring the Moon

AFTER Apollo 11, five more Apollo missions landed on the Moon. The last three missions brought along a special car, called the Lunar Roving Vehicle. Known as the Lunar Rover, or "Moon buggy," this battery-powered car helped the astronauts drive for miles over the Moon to collect rock and soil samples and explore its dusty surface.

The Rover had a TV camera so people on Earth could see what the astronauts saw. Viewers discovered an amazing variety of terrain, including lunar plains, canyons, and craters. The astronauts worked outside for several hours a day, exploring, doing scientific experiments, and collecting samples.

All together, the Apollo astronauts collected 855 pounds of rock in many different sizes. One discovery was a rock found to be over four billions years old. Called the "genesis rock," it was thought to be part of the Moon's original crust. Such geological clues helped scientists unlock many secrets of the Moon's past.

◀ Rock Collecting

To gather lunar rocks, the astronauts had special equipment. These included a map book, an airtight sample container, and collecting tongs. These were needed because the crew's space suits and gloves were so bulky it was hard to bend or pick things up easily.

HISTORY FACT: APOLLO 13

One Apollo mission was a close call. In 1970, Apollo 13 was heading toward the Moon when an explosion occurred in the spacecraft. The crew managed to survive by climbing into their lunar module "lifeboat" and just barely returned safely to Earth.

▶ Moon Treasure

Back on Earth, three laboratory technicians study a basketball-size lunar rock. It was one of some 2,000 samples of rock, stones, sand, dust, and other material collected by Apollo crews.

▼ Lunar Rover

The Lunar Rover was made of lightweight metal, mainly aluminum. It had wire mesh tires to grip the dusty lunar surface. The battery-powered car had a TV camera, umbrella-shaped antenna, and tool rack. It could travel 7 miles an hour. In it, the astronauts explored many miles from base.

▼ Taking Samples

Apollo 12 astronaut Alan Bean holds a special metal sample container filled with lunar soil. His visor reflects astronaut Pete Conrad, who took the picture. The samples the Apollo astronauts brought back helped scientists learn about the history of both the Moon and the solar system.

A Different World

LATER Apollo crews stayed for longer periods and saw even more of the Moon. From their lunar modules, they photographed the lunar surface. This helped experts create more accurate maps of the Moon. They also drove over the Moon's surface and collected many more samples.

As they worked, the crews became accustomed to the starkness and forbidding extremes of the lunar environment. Temperatures may range from over 200 degrees below zero to 200 degrees above zero Fahrenheit. Yet the astronauts also found that the Moon is a strangely beautiful world, with lunar canyons, mountains, and valleys. It has no wind or rain and is eerily silent because there is no air to transmit sound. The astronauts talked to one another by radios in their helmets. They also described many of the remarkable things they saw to people listening on Earth.

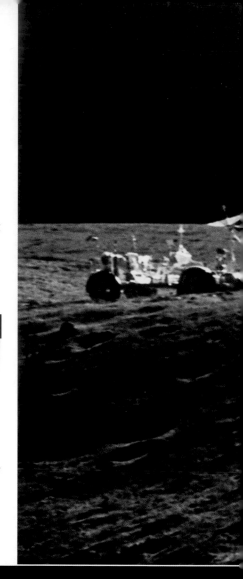

► CHECKING OUT A CRATER

Apollo 16 astronaut John Young looks for rock samples near North Ray Crater. About three-fourths of a mile wide and 650 feet deep, this was the largest crater the astronauts explored.

FUN FACT: LASTING FOOTPRINTS

Because of the Moon's weak gravity, it cannot hold air or water, as does the Earth. There is no wind or rain to blow or wash away a footprint. The Apollo crews' footprints may stay for millions of years.

▼ MOON BASE

This panorama shows the Apollo 16 home base on the Moon. The Lunar Rover sits parked near the lunar module, with the American flag placed nearby. The astronauts explored in the Lunar Rover and returned to the module to rest.

◄ ROCK HUNT

Apollo 16 astronaut Charles Duke looks for samples at Station 1, an exploration site. At left, a famous makeshift golf club was swung by Apollo 14 astronaut Alan Shepard just before he left the Moon. The Moon's gravity, one-sixth that of Earth's, helped him hit two balls 200 and 400 yards.

Homeward Bound

APOLLO 17 was the last mission to visit the Moon. At the end of the mission in 1972, the astronauts left behind a plaque. It signaled the end of the human Moon explorations. When the astronauts climbed into their lunar module and left for home, they had completed a great adventure and an important job.

A total of 12 men landed on the Moon. They gathered a vast store of knowledge. From rock and soil samples, scientists learned about the Moon's formation, history, and chemistry. They discovered that Moon minerals are similar to Earth's but many have heavier iron and titanium content. They found the Moon has a very thin atmosphere of helium, hydrogen, argon, and neon. They also found that the Moon has a magnetic field.

Considered one of the greatest scientific achievements of human history, Apollo established the United States as the world leader in space technology. It also began an exciting new era of exploring the frontiers of space.

▲ "Wish You Were Here"
Apollo 16 astronaut Charles Duke put a picture of his family down on the Moon's surface and photographed it. He also named a crater on the Moon, Cat Crater, for "Charles and Tom," his two sons.

FUN FACT: LONG WAY FROM HOME
The Moon's distance from Earth is about 239,000 miles. Apollo 11 took a total of four days to get to the Moon, traveling at speeds of up to 24,182 miles an hour.

▲ Moon Crossing
Above, the Apollo 12 lunar module moves across the Moon in a picture taken from the orbiting command and service module. Below, the Apollo 16 command and service module glides over lunar craters in a picture taken from the lunar module.

➤ Destination Earth
Earth appears over the Moon as Apollo 11's *Eagle* leaves the lunar surface. This dramatic shot was taken by Michael Collins on the command and service module *Columbia*. Minutes later, *Eagle* docked with *Columbia* to make the return trip to Earth.

Skylab

S KYLAB, the first U.S. space station, was built after the Apollo missions. It was launched May 14, 1973. The size of a small house, Skylab measured 118 feet long. Built from part of an empty Saturn V rocket, it had living and work space for three astronauts, solar panels for power, and telescopes to study the Sun and Earth.

A "laboratory in the sky," Skylab's main goal was to learn if astronauts could survive in space for long periods. Three crews lived in Skylab from 1973 to 1974 for up to 84 days. Orbiting the Earth every 93 minutes at 17,000 miles an hour, they ate, slept, and worked in zero gravity, or weightlessness. Because muscles weaken without gravity, they exercised daily. Mission Control constantly monitored their bodies. The tests showed the crews remained healthy. In Skylab, they performed hundreds of experiments and took thousands of photographs of the Sun and Earth. Skylab was a big success. Later abandoned, it fell from orbit in 1979.

▲ DINNER IS SERVED
Skylab's crew ate a variety of fresh and frozen foods, heated on this warming tray. Forks, spoons, and knives had magnets to keep them from floating away. Food had plastic covers. The crew ate by a window to enjoy the view.

▶ HOME IN SPACE
Skylab, the first U.S. space station, orbits Earth 270 miles high. Launched in 1973, the station was a laboratory and home to three crews of astronauts through 1974. Winglike solar panels converted the Sun's energy for power.

94

SPACE SPIDER

Can spiders spin webs in the weightless conditions of space? To find out, Skylab took along spider passengers. This spider named Arabella (left) was confused and could not spin well for two days. Then, she adjusted and spun normal webs.

PULLING POWER

In the weightlessness of space, human body fluids drift up to the upper body. Astronaut Owen Garriott tests a machine called the Lower Body Negative Pressure experiment. It corrects the problem by pulling fluids back down to the legs.

LIFE ON SKYLAB

Owen Garriott gives fellow astronaut Alan Bean a haircut. A suction hose collects the hair so it won't float away. At Christmas, Skylab astronauts decorated their space home with a Christmas tree made of food cans.

INSIDE STORY

A cutaway of Skylab's orbital workshop reveals its two sections. At top was a laboratory where the crew worked on scientific experiments. Below, the living quarters had a shower, toilet, galley, and eating and sleeping areas.

Apollo-Soyuz

I N the 1970s, the United States and the Soviet Union began a new period of cooperation. They even agreed to launch a joint space mission, called the Apollo-Soyuz Test Project. In July 1975, two manned spacecraft took off. One was an American Apollo capsule launched from Florida. The other, a Soyuz capsule, was launched from Kazakhstan in the Soviet Union. On July 17, the two capsules met in Earth orbit and successfully docked. They used a specially designed docking module. It fit to the Apollo on one end and to the Soyuz on the other end.

After docking, the two crews met, shook hands, and visited each other's ships. They talked and ate together, and also did experiments in astronomy together. The spacecraft remained docked together for two days. Both returned safely to Earth. With this historic meeting, the two countries began to help each other in using space for peaceful purposes.

▲ Taking Off

Soyuz 19 lifts off on July 15, 1975. Two days later it would rendezvous with Apollo in Earth orbit.

▼ ◄ Famous Fliers

Laika, a little dog, was the first living creature in space. She was launched in 1957 in Sputnik II. A portrait of Soviet cosmonauts includes left to right: Pavel Popovich, Yuri Gagarin, Valentina Tereshkova, Valery Bykovsky, Andrian Nikolayev, and Gherman Titov. Yuri Gagarin was the first person to fly in space. Mementos at left include his Communist Party card and a medal.

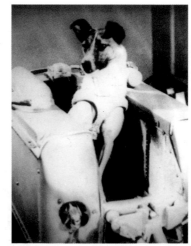

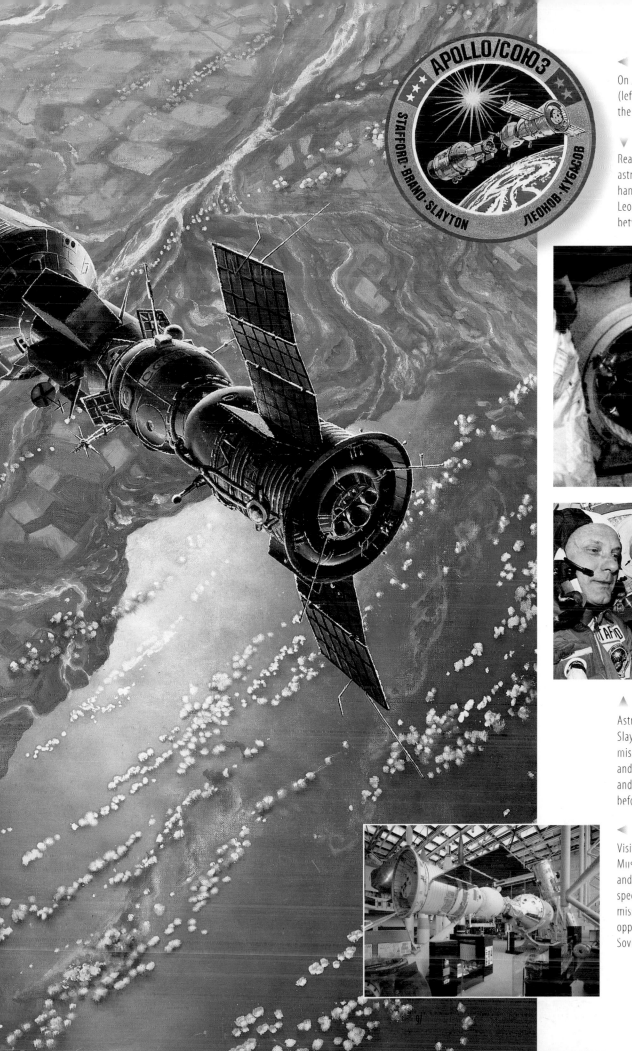

◄ Apollo Meets Soyuz

On July 17, 1975, a U.S. Apollo spacecraft (left) docks with the Soviet Soyuz over the Caspian Sea.

▼ "Hello!"

Reaching through the hatch, American astronaut Thomas Stafford (right) shakes hands with Soviet cosmonaut Aleksey Leonov. The mission symbolized goodwill between the two nations.

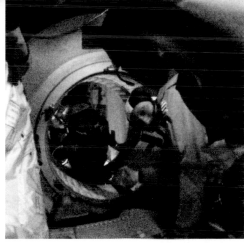

▲ A Toast

Astronauts Thomas Stafford and Donald Slayton celebrate the success of their mission by drinking a toast. The American and Soviet crews exchanged greetings and visited each other's craft four times before returning home.

◄ Apollo-Soyuz On Display

Visitors to the National Air and Space Museum can see a replica of the Apollo and Soyuz spacecraft docked with the special docking adapter built for the mission. The display gives a good opportunity to compare U.S. and Soviet spacecraft.

Space Suits

▼ SR-71 PRESSURE SUIT

Pilots of the Lockheed SR-71 Blackbird reconnaissance jet flew at 85,300 feet. At that altitude, they had to wear pressure suits much like those worn by astronauts. The suit provided normal air pressure around the pilot and oxygen to breathe.

WHEN astronauts venture outside their spacecraft to explore or work in space, they must be well protected. Otherwise they would quickly die in the hostile environment of space. A space suit is the astronaut's protection and life support system. Going outside the spacecraft is called an EVA (extravehicular activity). Wearing a space suit, the astronaut can survive up to 8 hours.

Early space suits were bulky, with up to 15 layers of material, and uncomfortable to move in. Today's suits have layers of light, airtight material such as nylon and Teflon. They protect against extreme heat or cold and against the destructive impact of tiny particles called micrometeoroids.

The space suit provides oxygen, a waste removal system, and radio communication. Astronauts can also move freely by attaching a chairlike jetpack called the MMU (Manned Maneuvering Unit). It is propelled by small gas-jet motors called thrusters. The astronaut controls them with buttons, much like video game controls.

▲ EARLY PILOT'S SUIT

Flying at altitudes over 10,000 feet, early pilots had to breathe oxygen through face masks to survive in the thin air aloft. Above, pilot Wiley Post developed the first practical pressure suit for making his record high-altitude flight in 1935.

▲ MAN OR ROCKET?

Designed in 1960, this early space suit called the "tripod teepee" was not a success. A rigid metal cylinder with holes for the arms and legs, it was bulky and inflexible. The wearer here could hardly move his arms to use tools and could not bend over or sit normally.

▲ MERCURY SPACE SUIT

This space suit was worn by Gordon Cooper, one of America's first astronauts. The suit had an aluminized nylon covering and 13 zippers for a snug fit. The gloves had tiny finger lights to help the astronaut see controls and charts.

◀ EMU

The space suit the shuttle astronauts wear to work in space is the EMU, or Extravehicular Mobility Unit. It provides air, protection from severe heat or cold, and communication. Adding a jet-powered Manned Maneuvering Unit (MMU), the astronaut can move around freely outside.

1. TV camera
2. Sun visor
3. Lights to see in dark
4. Microphone for communication
5. Backpack with oxygen
6. Tool tether to keep tools from floating away
7. Procedure check list
8. Harness to hold jetpack in place
9. MMU hand control to fire thrusters for movement
10. Safety tethers
11. Tough outer fabric to protect against tears
12. Aluminum mylar layer for warmth
13. Underwear with water tubing to cool body
14. Coated nylon protective layer
15. Gas-powered thrusters on MMU jetpack

▲ SUITED UP

Shuttle crew members wear launch-and-entry suits as they head for the launch pad. The suit provides pressure to protect against "G" forces. Once in the spacecraft, they put on helmets, seal the visors, and use the suits' oxygen supplies, keeping themselves safe in case of a loss of cabin pressure.

The Space Shuttle

THE space shuttle is the world's only reusable spacecraft. It was developed after the huge expense of the Apollo missions. Those craft were used only once. The space shuttle can be reused over and over. It consists of three parts: 1) the orbiter, an airplane-like body with three engines, 2) an external tank to fuel the engines at liftoff, and 3) two solid rocket boosters for extra energy at liftoff. The shuttle is launched like a rocket, orbits the Earth like a spacecraft, and lands like a glider.

The first shuttle to fly in space was *Columbia*. It lifted off on April 12, 1981, with astronauts John Young and Robert Crippen. "T-Minus 5...4...3...2...1 Ignition!" *Columbia*'s engines roared to life and it blasted into the sky. Twelve minutes later it was circling the Earth 200 miles high. The flight lasted 54 hours and made 36 Earth orbits. All systems performed well. The astronauts were thrilled with the two-day ride. After returning safely to Earth, John Young said, "We are really not that far...from going to the stars."

FUN FACT: FAST RIDE

The space shuttle zooms in orbit around the Earth at 5 miles a second. That's over 10 times as fast as a speeding rifle bullet!

▲ FAST EXIT

In case of emergency before launch, the crew exit the shuttle in a slidewire basket. Shuttle *Endeavour* mission specialists practice the exit. As Michael Foale pulls a lever to release the basket, Claude Nicollier and John Grunsfeld watch.

▶ LIFTOFF!

Riding columns of fire, *Columbia* rises April 12, 1981 in its first historic flight. Above, the shuttle *Discovery* travels to the launch pad on the world's biggest tracked vehicle, called the crawler.

"Man, that was one fantastic ride!"
—Robert L. Crippen, pilot shuttle *Columbia*, April 12, 1981

Keeping Safe

The space shuttle, the most complex machine ever built, has more than 600,000 parts. At launch, the orbiter's Space Shuttle Main Engines (SSMEs) ignite, drawing 760 tons of liquid fuel at a rate of 1,000 gallons a second from the huge orange External Tank (ET). The SSMEs and SRBs deliver 6.5 million pounds of thrust to launch the vehicle into orbit.

The shuttle reenters Earth's atmosphere at twenty-five times the speed of sound. Frictional heating generates temperatures of more than 3,000 degrees Fahrenheit. Thousands of silica tiles on the shuttle shield it from this scorching heat. The shuttle's nose and the leading edges of the wing get even hotter; advanced materials protect them. In 2003, launch debris smashed a hole in the leading edge of *Columbia*'s left wing. Superheated air later forced itself into the craft during reentry, destroying her and killing her crew of seven. Since then, every shuttle mission has scheduled careful on-orbit inspection of the heat shield before return to Earth.

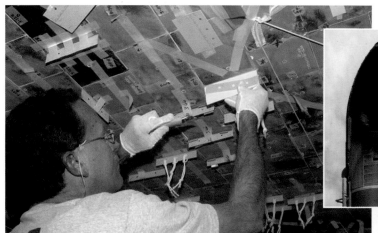

▲ Shuttle Surgery

A technician cuts away excess gap filler from the silica tiles that form *Discovery*'s heat shield. Two fillers had stuck out on a flight, and engineers feared that such variations could produce dangerous damage to the shield. Astronauts photograph the big External Tank after separation (inset) to spot any problems for correction before the next mission.

▶ We Deliver

Photographed from the International Space Station, the *Discovery* proudly displays her payload-bay full of parts and equipment for use aboard the station. A typical payload would include food, water, and clothing plus such hardware as station parts, spacewalk tools—and crew replacements.

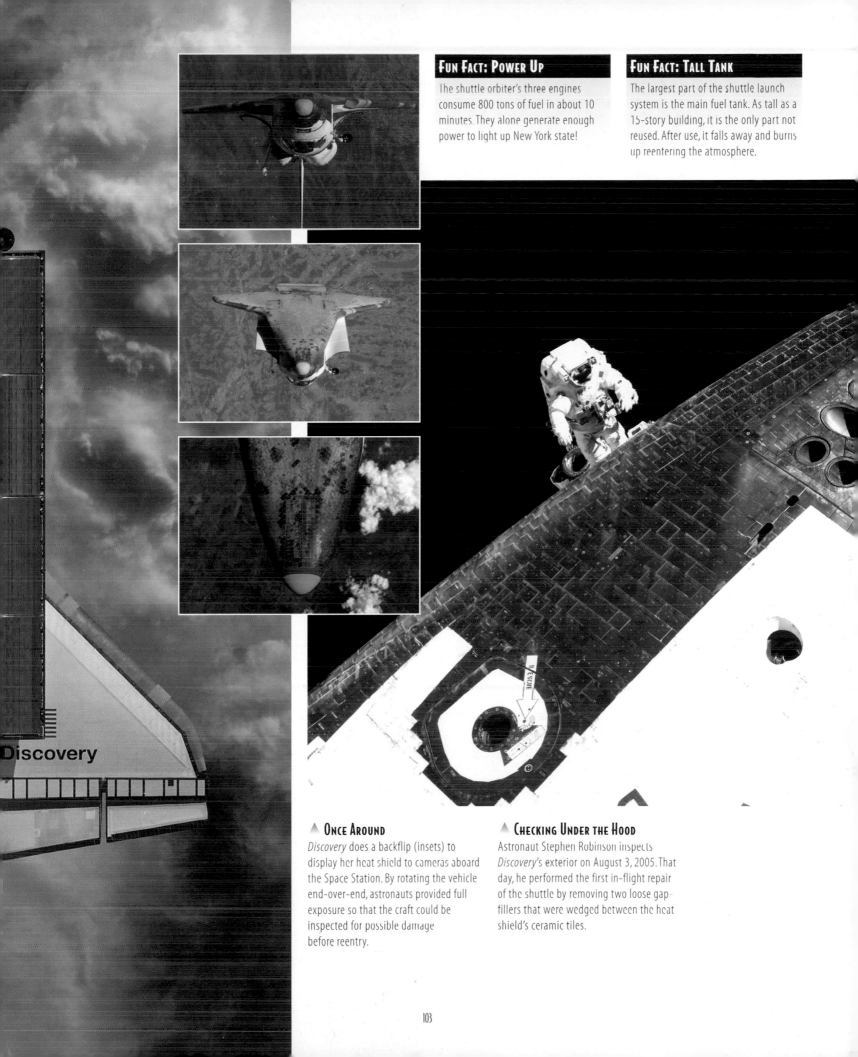

Discovery

FUN FACT: POWER UP

The shuttle orbiter's three engines consume 800 tons of fuel in about 10 minutes. They alone generate enough power to light up New York state!

FUN FACT: TALL TANK

The largest part of the shuttle launch system is the main fuel tank. As tall as a 15-story building, it is the only part not reused. After use, it falls away and burns up reentering the atmosphere.

▲ ONCE AROUND

Discovery does a backflip (insets) to display her heat shield to cameras aboard the Space Station. By rotating the vehicle end-over-end, astronauts provided full exposure so that the craft could be inspected for possible damage before reentry.

▲ CHECKING UNDER THE HOOD

Astronaut Stephen Robinson inspects *Discovery*'s exterior on August 3, 2005. That day, he performed the first in-flight repair of the shuttle by removing two loose gap-fillers that were wedged between the heat shield's ceramic tiles.

103

The Glass Cockpit

THIS is the space shuttle cockpit, located on the flight deck. It is the main control area of the spacecraft. In this picture, the seats have been removed. Two spaces for seats face the orbiter's front windows. The mission commander sits on the left and the pilot on the right. Either one can control the craft from his seat. Flying the shuttle requires a vast array of instruments. Over 2,100 different controls line the cockpit. The new shuttle cockpit has more computer screens, and so it is called the "glass cockpit."

The flight deck and rest of the crew cabin are pressurized so the crew do not need space suits once in orbit. They float around in weightlessness, often called "zero G," inside the cabin. From the flight deck, the crew can control other parts of the spacecraft. They can open and close the payload, or cargo, bay doors. They can move the shuttle's big robot arm to grasp and retrieve objects such as communications satellites in space. The shuttle's movements can be controlled manually by the crew and also by Mission Control in Houston.

FUN FACT: MORE INSTRUMENTS

The space shuttle cockpit has more than three times the number of instruments and controls required by the Apollo command modules that traveled to the Moon.

▲ PRACTICE MAKES PERFECT

Astronaut Brent Jett, in a simulator that duplicates the real Shuttle cockpit, runs through post-launch procedures. As a safety precaution, astronauts wear pressure suits during launch and reentry.

▼ **CONTROL CENTER**
Inside the cockpit of the shuttle *Columbia*,
instrument switches and other controls
cover the walls. The complex system can be
operated by a single astronaut. Closed circuit
TV monitors give the crew live pictures of
activities in the ship and outside.

Shuttle Orbiter

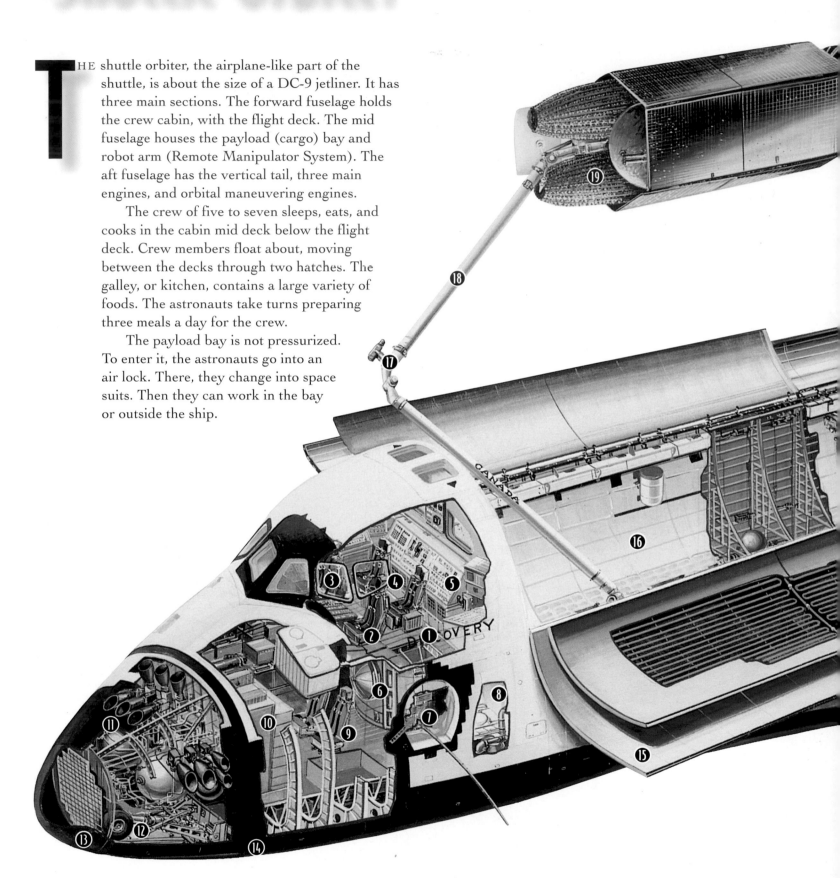

THE shuttle orbiter, the airplane-like part of the shuttle, is about the size of a DC-9 jetliner. It has three main sections. The forward fuselage holds the crew cabin, with the flight deck. The mid fuselage houses the payload (cargo) bay and robot arm (Remote Manipulator System). The aft fuselage has the vertical tail, three main engines, and orbital maneuvering engines.

The crew of five to seven sleeps, eats, and cooks in the cabin mid deck below the flight deck. Crew members float about, moving between the decks through two hatches. The galley, or kitchen, contains a large variety of foods. The astronauts take turns preparing three meals a day for the crew.

The payload bay is not pressurized. To enter it, the astronauts go into an air lock. There, they change into space suits. Then they can work in the bay or outside the ship.

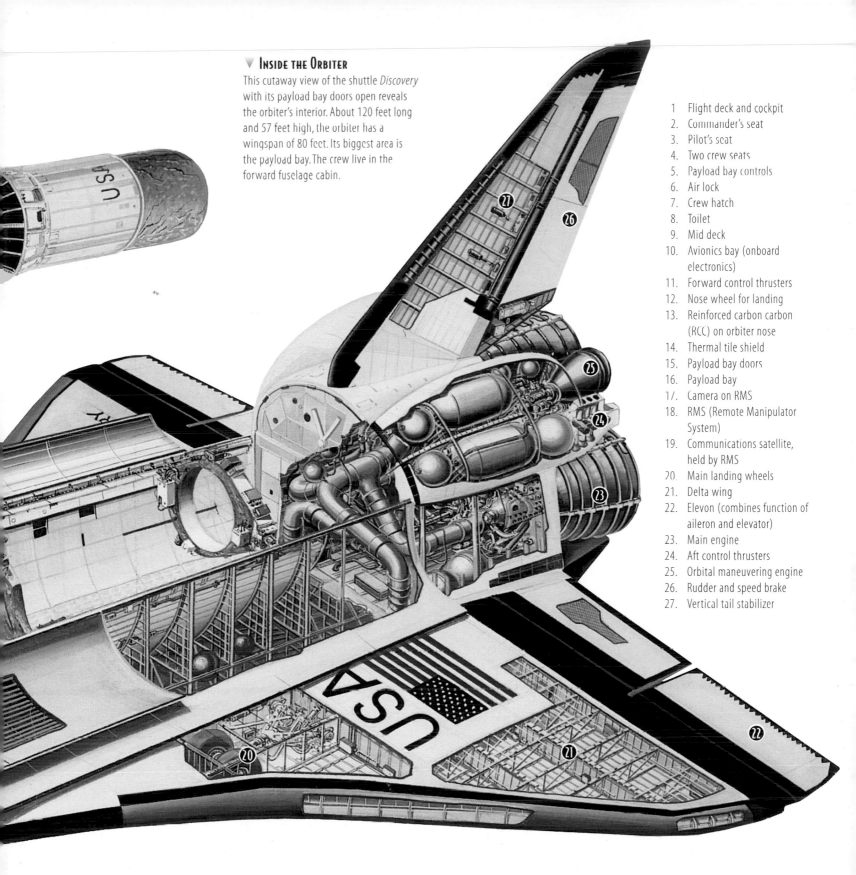

▼ Inside the Orbiter

This cutaway view of the shuttle *Discovery* with its payload bay doors open reveals the orbiter's interior. About 120 feet long and 57 feet high, the orbiter has a wingspan of 80 feet. Its biggest area is the payload bay. The crew live in the forward fuselage cabin.

1. Flight deck and cockpit
2. Commander's seat
3. Pilot's seat
4. Two crew seats
5. Payload bay controls
6. Air lock
7. Crew hatch
8. Toilet
9. Mid deck
10. Avionics bay (onboard electronics)
11. Forward control thrusters
12. Nose wheel for landing
13. Reinforced carbon carbon (RCC) on orbiter nose
14. Thermal tile shield
15. Payload bay doors
16. Payload bay
17. Camera on RMS
18. RMS (Remote Manipulator System)
19. Communications satellite, held by RMS
20. Main landing wheels
21. Delta wing
22. Elevon (combines function of aileron and elevator)
23. Main engine
24. Aft control thrusters
25. Orbital maneuvering engine
26. Rudder and speed brake
27. Vertical tail stabilizer

FUN FACT: BIG LOAD

The payload bay can hold over 60,000 pounds, or 30 tons, of cargo, including space station parts, satellites, telescopes, Spacelab, a portable science laboratory, or other equipment.

Space Telescope

S PACE shuttle missions, which last usually one to two weeks, often launch equipment in space, retrieve it, or repair it. In 1990, the space shuttle *Discovery* launched the huge Hubble Space Telescope (HST) into Earth orbit. Called the "new window on the universe," it was expected to give much clearer pictures of space than ever before because it would be orbiting outside Earth's atmosphere.

Unfortunately, the first images from the HST were blurred because of a faulty mirror system. After over a year of training, crew in the space shuttle *Endeavour* took off to repair the telescope in December 1993.

The astronauts worked on the telescope standing on the shuttle's big robot arm, the Remote Manipulator System. They replaced corrective optical equipment, added a new camera, and other parts. By January, images from the telescope showed the repairs had worked. The pictures were clear and spectacular! These images have helped scientists learn much more about the universe.

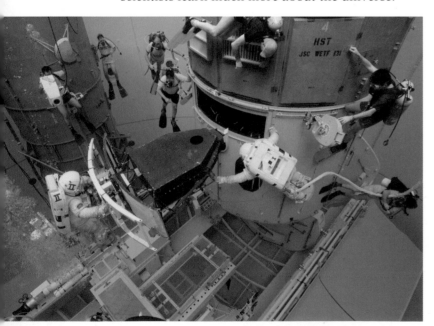

▲ Underwater Training

Astronauts prepare for a mission to repair the Hubble Space Telescope in space by training in a huge tank of water. The feeling of moving in water is similar to that of floating in the weightlessness of space.

◄ Eye Care

Astronauts work on the Hubble Space Telescope (left and inset), improving the sight of the "Eye on the Universe." Service missions, which began in 1992, extend the life of this vital space-studying tool.

▼ Unseen Now Seen

From the Hubble Space Telescope's camera comes a sight never seen before—spirals of interstellar "dust" in a halo of light around a star 20,000 light-years from Earth, the edge of our Milky Way galaxy.

FUN FACT: EYE IN THE SKY

Looking at stars through telescopes on Earth is hard since the atmosphere distorts the image. Orbiting 370 miles above the Earth, the Hubble Space Telescope gets a much clearer view.

▲ Spiraling Space

The Hubble camera snaps a swirling galaxy 3,300 light-years away. Astronomers call it a barred spiral galaxy, different from others because its arms do not spiral into the center but connect to a straight "bar" of stars.

Meeting Mir

ON June 29, 1995, the space shuttle *Atlantis* made a historic flight. It successfully met and docked with the Russian space station Mir, or "Peace," orbiting 245 miles above the Earth. Shuttle mission commander Robert L. Gibson steered *Atlantis* into docking position near Mir. Both were hurtling through space at 17,500 miles an hour. Gibson had to slow *Atlantis* down and very carefully maneuver it to avoid a crash. He also had to act quickly enough to catch and lock onto the space station before it drifted beyond reach. He performed the maneuver perfectly.

After docking, the *Atlantis* crew floated through a connecting tunnel to enter Mir and met the Russian cosmonauts inside. For five days, the two crews socialized and worked on experiments together. This was the first of several visits of space shuttles to Mir. The two countries that were once fierce rivals in space have since done much to cooperate with each other to increase space knowledge.

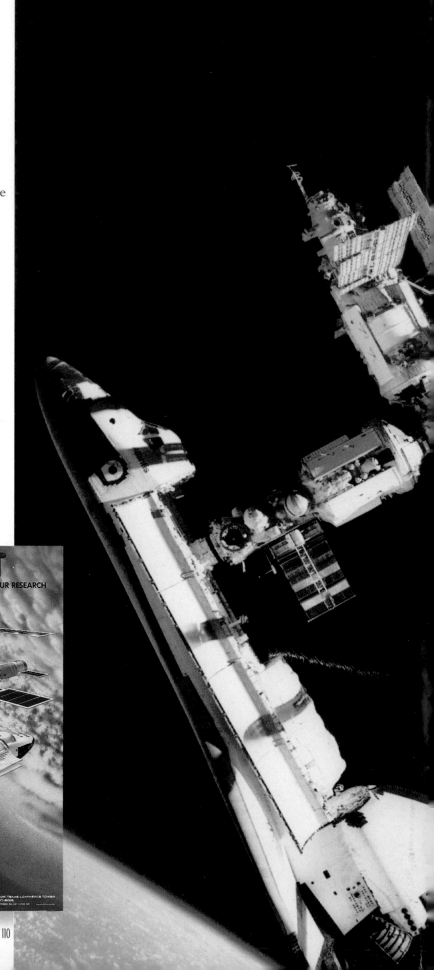

▲ Space Partners

A mission patch for a 1996 Shuttle-Mir mission emphasizes the cooperation between the two nations in peaceful space projects. At right, a poster promotes the rental of space on Mir to American research companies.

▶ ▶ Linked Together

Docked in space, the shuttle *Atlantis* and Mir space station float in orbit. This picture was taken by a Soyuz ferry spacecraft in June 1995. Such joint missions helped pave the way for work on the new International Space Station.

FUN FACT: LONG TRIP

The record time for living in space is held by Russian doctor Valeri Poliakov. He stayed on Mir a total of 438 days! From his experience, scientists learned much about how the human body adapts to long periods in space.

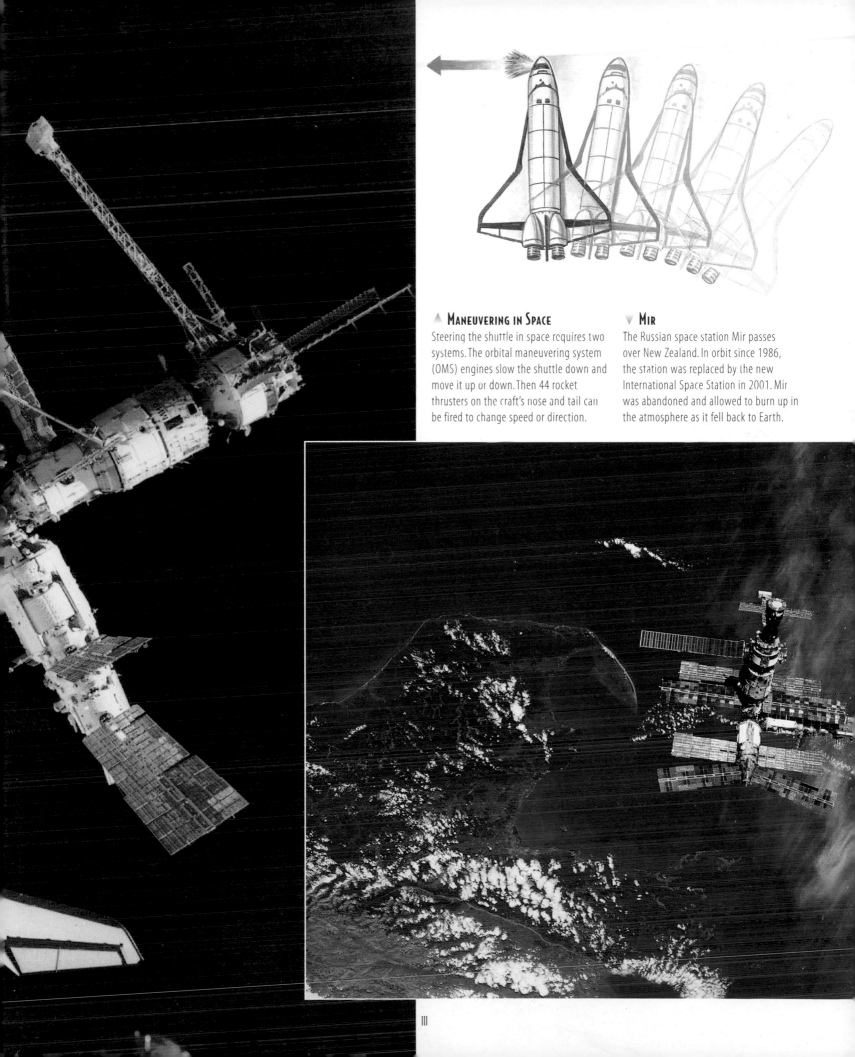

▲ MANEUVERING IN SPACE

Steering the shuttle in space requires two systems. The orbital maneuvering system (OMS) engines slow the shuttle down and move it up or down. Then 44 rocket thrusters on the craft's nose and tail can be fired to change speed or direction.

▼ MIR

The Russian space station Mir passes over New Zealand. In orbit since 1986, the station was replaced by the new International Space Station in 2001. Mir was abandoned and allowed to burn up in the atmosphere as it fell back to Earth.

Living in Space

SPACE BEAR
Magellan T. Bear became the first official teddy bear in space when he flew aboard the shuttle *Discovery* in 1995. Sponsored by a group of school children, he was an "education specialist."

W HAT'S it like to blast into space and fly on the space shuttle? Do you get sick? How do you use the bathroom? What do you eat? How do you sleep? These are all questions astronauts are often asked.

Most astronauts are very excited at liftoff and they enjoy the free feeling of weightless-ness in space. Some are a little space sick at first, but soon adjust to the lack of gravity. They learn to glide, twist, and somersault expertly through space.

The crew eat the same foods and drinks they enjoy on Earth, including fruits, vegetables, meats, and desserts, but they eat them from disposable containers. The astronauts do not shower because water would escape and float in blobs everywhere. Instead, they squirt water on a sponge and take sponge baths. The shuttle has a bathroom and special toilet the crew use.

To sleep, the astronauts curl up inside sleeping bags hung on a wall or simply float in a comfortable spot.

SPACE TOILET
Astronauts aboard the shuttle use this special toilet. It has air suction in place of gravity to remove wastes through a hose and bowl. It also has foot restraints so the astronaut using it won't float away!

MISSION PATCHES
Space shuttle mission patches have a design symbolizing each mission and the names of astronauts on the mission.

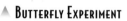

BUTTERFLY EXPERIMENT
These Painted Lady butterflies emerged from cocoons on a space shuttle mission. They were an experiment planned by a group of high school students to see if caterpillars can develop in the microgravity of space.

YOUNG · CRIPPEN

LOUSMA · FULLERTON
COLUMBIA

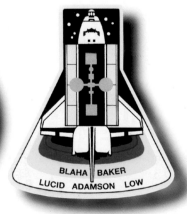

BLAHA BAKER
LUCID ADAMSON LOW

CHILTON BRANDENSTEIN MELNICK
endeavour
THUOT HIEB THORNTON AKERS

▼ Moving in Space

Mission specialist Carl Walz floats through a tunnel from the shuttle cabin into a science laboratory module. Although astronauts often feel nausea at first, they soon enjoy moving in space. Many say it feels like swimming in air.

▶ Brushing Up

Astronauts Frank Culbertson and Daniel Bursch brush their teeth on the shuttle. They use disposable brushes with edible toothpaste and squirt water in their mouths. There is no sink or running water because the water would float around the cabin.

"The best part of being in space is being weightless. It feels wonderful to be able to float without effort... it's pure fun..."

—Astronaut Sally Ride describing life on the space shuttle in her book, *To Space and Back*

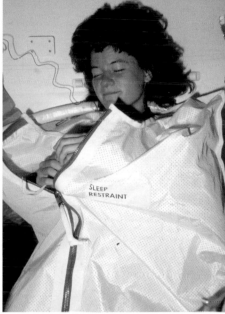

SLEEP RESTRAINT

▲ Sally K. Ride (1951–)

Sally Ride became the first American woman in space in 1983. Trained as a physicist, she joined NASA in 1978 and became an astronaut. She flew on the space shuttle *Challenger* as a mission specialist. Here, she sleeps in a sleeping restraint on the shuttle.

Gliding Home

RETURNING to Earth, the shuttle orbiter is transformed from a spacecraft into a giant glider. First, its maneuvering engine rockets fire a last time to slow it down to drop from orbit.

Reentering Earth's atmosphere, it passes through scorching heat and tremendous friction. The thermal heat shield does its job well and protects the ship during the fiery journey. Next, computers guide the orbiter through a series of S turns to slow it down more. The orbiter's speed drops from over 17,000 miles an hour to about 350 miles an hour.

The craft glides in silently. At about 20 miles from the runway, the mission commander takes control and brings it in for a landing. The shuttle can also land automatically, if necessary. As the wheels touch down, the craft lands at between 200 and 226 miles an hour and slows to a stop. Then the astronauts exit the orbiter on ordinary aircraft landing steps.

FUN FACT: MISSION NAMES

The official name of the space shuttle is the Space Transportation System. Each mission is named with the letters STS and a number, such as STS 1.

▶ Coming in to Land

Like a giant bird, the shuttle *Columbia* glides unpowered to land at Kennedy Space Center. The commander aims carefully landing the craft. If it misses the runway, he cannot turn around to come back and try again.

▶ What a Drag

Once the shuttle's wheels hit the runway, a parachute opens to slow the orbiter. As the craft lands at over 200 miles an hour, the drag chute helps it gradually brake to a stop.

▶ Getting a Lift

The shuttle *Atlantis* is lifted in a machine to mount it on the back of a Boeing 747. With no power to fly through the atmosphere after it lands, the shuttle orbiter must be ferried by a 747 back to its launch site.

▶ Piggyback Ride

Aboard a 747 ferry, the shuttle *Atlantis* returns to Florida after being repaired in California. Shuttles are used over and over, always launching from Kennedy Space Center in Florida.

Space station

THE largest object ever built in space, the International Space Station (ISS) floats in Earth orbit. Begun in 1996, the ISS has 18,000 cubic feet of living and working space. ISS builders include the United States, Russia, Canada, countries that belong to the European Space Agency, and Japan, whose contribution is an experiment module, the nation's first human space facility.

The station has a roomy kitchen, bathroom, and sleeping and exercise areas. Giant solar panels—270 feet in width—convert energy from the Sun for electric power. The station provides an international center for many kinds of scientific research. One, for example, is aimed at finding the best kind of food for astronauts. In its laboratories, scientists study life in space and test new medicines and materials for life on Earth. Someday, the ISS may also be the departure terminal for missions to other planets.

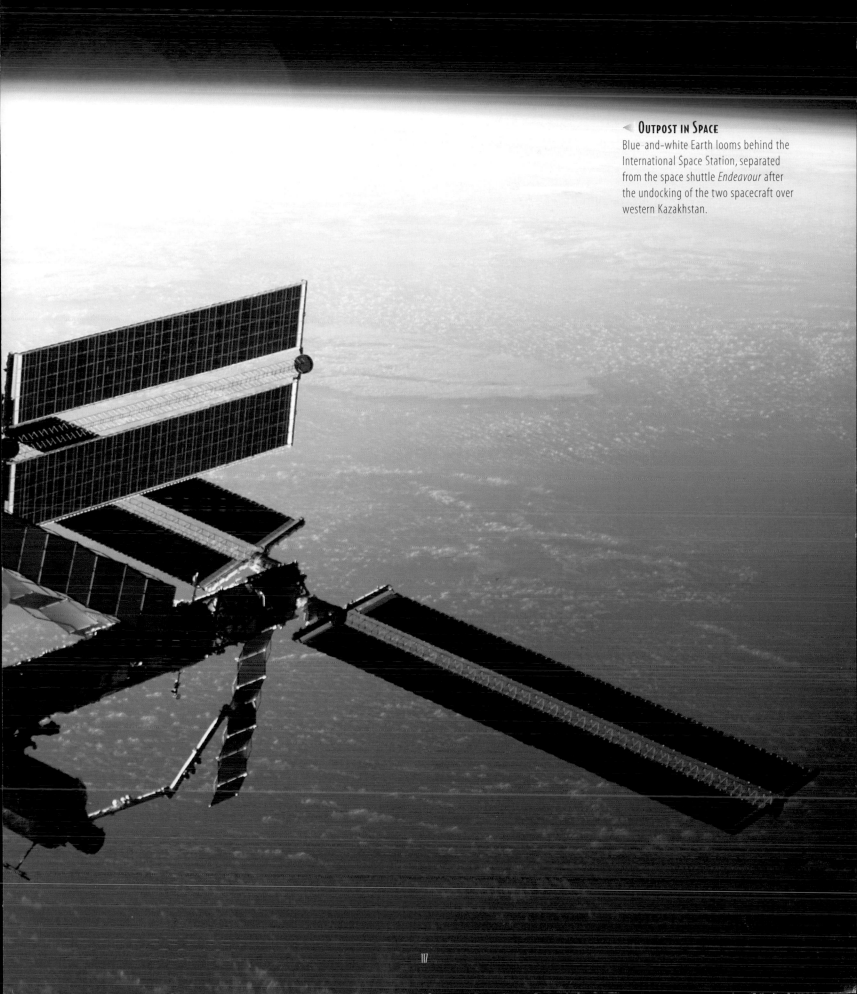

Blue-and-white Earth looms behind the
International Space Station, separated
from the space shuttle *Endeavour* after
the undocking of the two spacecraft over
western Kazakhstan.

Building the ISS

S OME 220 miles over Earth, the world's highest construction site bustles with activity. Workers ride cranes and hoist huge components into place. The giant structure that is going up is the International Space Station (ISS). The workers building it are astronauts.

The construction work will go on for years. The astronauts will spend many hours in EVAs (extravehicular activity), or spacewalks, assembling the station.

The absence of gravity on the station will allow scientists to do experiments not possible on Earth. Life on the ISS will also provide knowledge for future long-duration space travel beyond Earth's orbit. Astronauts in space experience loss of bone density and are exposed to radiation. Before astronauts head off on years-long journeys to other planets, scientists and doctors will need to learn much more about these and other medical effects of prolonged spaceflight—and how to counteract them.

▲ At Arm's Length

Shuttle astronaut Stephen K. Robinson hitches a ride on the station's Canadarm2 as he moves from one worksite to another outside the space station. Bigger and smarter than the first robotic arm, Canadarm2 is nearly 58 feet long and has seven motorized joints.

▲ Women in High Places

EVA astronaut Heidemarie M. Stefanyshyn-Piper (top, above) works on a station assembly task. Wendy B. Lawrence and James M. Kelly (above) operate the station's robot arm. Women have piloted and commanded the shuttle, and lived aboard the ISS.

▶ Hard Hat on High

David A. Wolf rides Canadarm2 during a construction spacewalk. The robot arm can maneuver huge components around the station, ride the length of the station on a mini-rail car, and even "walk", end over end, from one part of the station to another.

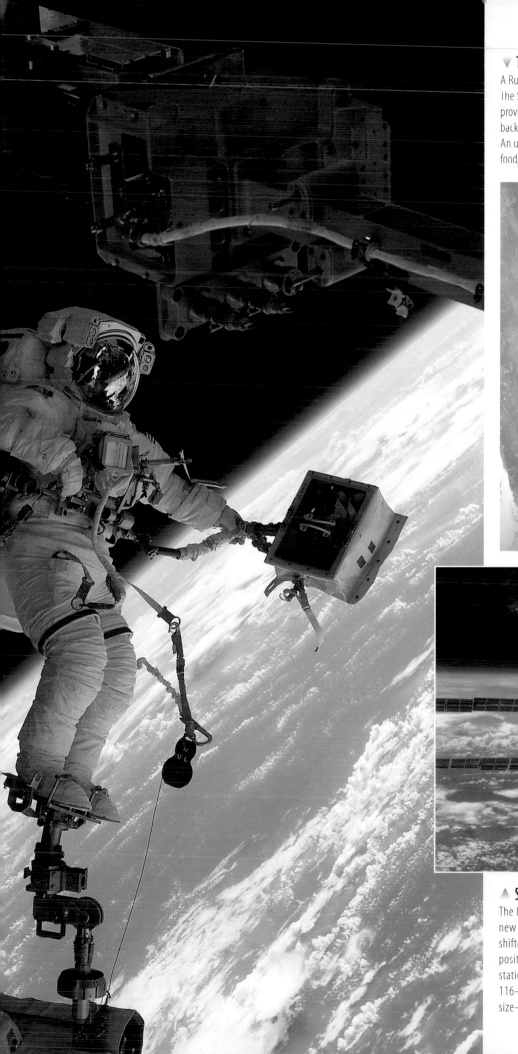

▼ THE RUSSIANS ARE COMING

A Russian Soyuz spacecraft approaches the ISS. The Soyuz is a vital link in the ISS system, and provided the only means of transporting people back and forth when the Shuttle was grounded. An unmanned Soyuz variant called *Progress* brings food, water and rocket propellant to the ISS.

▲ SOME ASSEMBLY REQUIRED

The ISS will keep growing and changing as new modules are brought into orbit and shifted about from interim to permanent positions. Compare this 2002 view of the station with the image from 2006 on pages 116-117. The station has about doubled in size—and will double again by 2010.

New Horizons

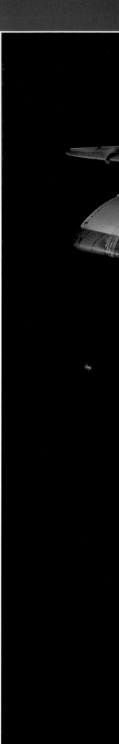

WHAT will flight in the future be like? How will tomorrow's space explorers travel? Take a look at SpaceShipOne, which rockets through the middle of these pages. The historic 2004 flight proved that private industry could build spacecraft and carry paying passengers. "This is a milestone for humanity," said John Spencer, president of the Space Tourism Society.

SpaceShipOne inspired the founding of The Spaceship Company, which will build a fleet of sub-orbital spacecraft designed for commercial use, such as taking tourists into space. Keeping watch over safety standards is the Personal Spaceflight Federation, formed by executives of companies promoting space travel.

The Russian Space Agency has already gone into the tourist business, offering trips beyond Earth to anyone who can pass a physical and buy the $20 million ticket. There is a long waiting line.

For trips to the Moon and the planets, however, government-produced spacecraft are likely to be the vehicles that carry human and robotic explorers.

To the Winner

This trophy, symbol of the $10 million Ansari X Prize, went to the creators of SpaceShipOne. The prize, named after the sponsoring Ansari family, is modeled after the Orteig Prize, won by Charles Lindbergh in 1927 for the first non-stop New York-to-Paris flight.

Spaceflight Champ

SpaceShipOne soars to the edge of space, winning the Ansari X Prize by safely carrying a pilot and equivalent weight of two passengers up to 328,000 feet twice within 14 days. It is the first spacecraft built by a private firm.

Pioneering Passenger

Anousheh Ansari, the first woman to go into space as a private person, poses with Russia's Soyuz spacecraft. She joined the crew on a flight to the International Space Station, promoting the idea of space travel.

◄ Up, Up, and Away

"White Knight," the turbojet mothership, after climbing to about 50,000 feet, releases SpaceShipOne. An 84-second rocket burn sends the spacecraft on a trajectory—up nearly 70 miles, then down to a safe landing.

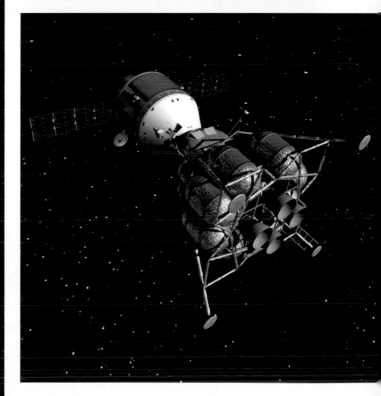

▲ Back to the Moon

NASA's plans for returning to the Moon focus on the Orion Crew Vehicle, its Ares I booster, and the unmanned Ares V booster. The Ares I is a five-segment solid rocket. The Orion capsule, carrying four to six astronauts, rides Ares I into orbit. In artists' conceptions of future flights, the Ares V cargo vehicle (top right) jettisons its fairing, exposing a lunar lander. In Earth orbit (center above), Orion docks with the lunar lander, still atop the Ares V upper stage. In Moon orbit (above) the lander casts off from Orion and heads for the surface.

Mission to Mars

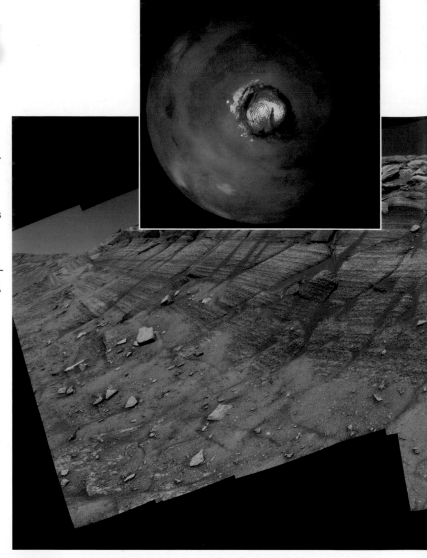

MARS, the red planet, has fascinated people for centuries. Mars's orbit lies about 42 million miles farther out from the Sun than Earth's. About half the size of our world, Mars has many Earthlike features, such as mountains, canyons, and polar ice caps. Yet Mars's air is 100 times thinner than Earth's and the planet is a freezing desert.

In 1976, two Viking landers touched down on Mars. In 1997, the Pathfinder mini-rover landed, followed by larger twin rovers, Spirit and Opportunity, in 2004. These craft showed Mars to be rocky and arid. Yet scientists believe Mars once had water that may have held microscopic life. Many think that Mars still hoards water underground. NASA's Mars Reconnaissance Orbiter has even found evidence of liquid water on the present-day Martian surface.

Where robots go, perhaps people can follow. A human mission to Mars could take about two years. The travelers would explore Mars for months, extracting oxygen from Mars's carbon dioxide atmosphere. They might find fossils, actual proof of other life in the universe. No one knows what lies in the future. Yet, as the story of flight has shown, tomorrow will be exciting as dreams become reality.

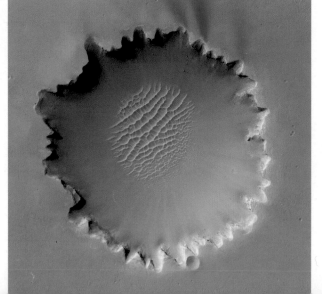

▲ EYES ON THE GROUND

The Mars Reconnaissance Orbiter (above) has sent back some of the best images ever taken from space. This image of Victoria Crater (right) is so sharp that the Mars rover Opportunity is visible in blow-ups. The widest notch in the crater, at the upper left, is Duck Bay and its northern edge, nearest the top of the image, is Cape Verde. Opportunity produced the image (upper right) from Duck Bay, looking toward Cape Verde. The image of the rover was later inserted to give a sense of scale.

122

◄ North Pole, Mars

The ice caps on Mars look a lot like the ones on Earth. But because Mars is so much colder than Earth, the ice caps are made of a mixture of water ice and "dry ice"—frozen carbon dioxide.

▼ Rover in the Picture

Opportunity took the 46 images used to create this composite. Then technicians on Earth inserted Opportunity herself into the shot so as to add a sense of scale and proportion to the final picture.

FUN FACT: PURE FICTION

In 1898, British author H.G. Wells wrote *The War of the Worlds*, a novel about creatures from Mars invading Earth. In 1938, the story was broadcast on radio. It was so convincing, many believed the invasion was real!

FUN FACT: SIGHTSEEING ON MARS

Visitors to Mars will see remarkable things. Mars has a volcano three times taller than Mount Everest and a huge canyon. It is four times deeper and ten times longer than the Grand Canyon.

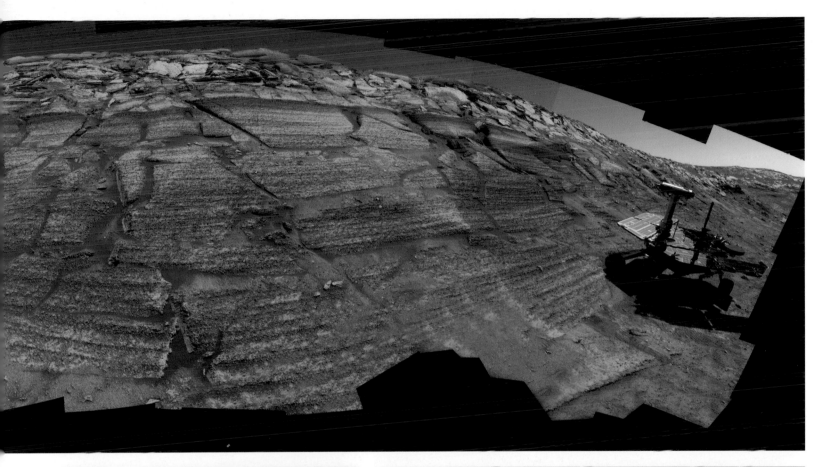

◄ Sand Trap

When Opportunity's six wheels all got stuck in a patch of loose soil, engineers on Earth (left, upper) reproduced the problem, then spent five weeks freeing the rover. The rover Spirit ground holes (left, lower) to test hardness and examine it.

▲ Roving Humans

Someday, there will be Mars rovers large enough to carry a driver and passengers. Serious plans for human visits to the Red Planet are just in the earliest stages. But some young reader of this book might be the first person to walk—and drive—on Mars.

Milestones of Flight

BEFORE 1900

1100– Chinese invent gunpowder
1300 and use early rockets as weapons

1300s Explorer Marco Polo reports human-carrying kites in China

1500 Leonardo da Vinci of Italy sketches early designs for flying machines

1783 First recorded human flight in a hot-air balloon invented by French brothers Joseph and Etienne Montgolfier

1783 Jacques Charles of France invents the hydrogen balloon

1804 Englishman Sir George Cayley invents and flies the first heavier-than-air craft, a model glider

1852 Henri Giffard of France invents and flies the first dirigible, powered by steam

1894 Steam-powered flying machine, *Leviathan*, rises several inches off the ground for a few seconds

1891 German engineer Otto Lilienthal becomes the first person to pilot gliders

1896 Lilienthal dies after a glider crash

1896 American Samuel P. Langley launches a large unmanned powered flying machine, a steam-driven model called an "Aerodrome"

1900

1900 Orville and Wilbur Wright fly their first glider

1903 The Wright brothers achieve the first controlled, powered flight in their airplane, the *Flyer*, going 120 feet in 12 seconds

1907 American inventor Glenn Curtiss forms his own aircraft manufacturing company

1907 Paul Cornu of France makes the first flight in a helicopter, hovering over 5 feet for 20 seconds

1908 Glenn Curtiss flies his plane *June*

Bug in the first public airplane flight in the United States

1908 The first airplane passenger, Charles W. Furnas, flies with Wilbur Wright

1909 Wilbur Wright goes to France and makes public demonstration flights

1908 The first airplane fatality occurs when Lt. Thomas Selfridge is killed in a crash riding with Orville Wright

1909 Frenchman Louis Blériot becomes the first to fly across the English Channel

1910

1910 Baroness Raymonde de Laroche of France is the first woman to earn a pilot's license

1911 Harriet Quimby becomes the first American woman to receive a pilot's license

1912 Cal Rodgers flies coast to coast across the United States in 84 days

1912 Harriet Quimby becomes the first woman to fly across the English Channel and later that year is killed in a flying accident

1913 The first Schneider Trophy Race for seaplanes is held in Monaco

1913 Russian inventor Igor Sikorsky builds and flies the first four-engine plane, the *Le Grand*

1914 First scheduled airline flights, of a flying-boat service from St. Petersburg to Tampa, Florida

1914–1918 World War I

1915 First fighter plane built with a machine gun synchronized to fire through spinning propeller blades, the Fokker Eindecker

1918 Baron Manfred von Richthofen, German ace known as the Red Baron, is shot down and killed

1918 First experimental airmail service in the United States

1919 British pilots John Alcock and Arthur Brown fly first nonstop flight across the Atlantic Ocean

1920

1920 First Pulitzer Trophy Race is held

1923 First nonstop transcontinental flight across the United States by Kelly and Macready in 26 hours and 50 minutes

1924 Douglas World Cruisers *Chicago* and *New Orleans* make the first round-the-world flight, in about six months

1926 Ford Tri-Motor is introduced

1926 American Robert H. Goddard launches the first successful liquid-propellant rocket

1926 Commander Richard Byrd of the U.S. Navy flies over the North Pole in a Fokker F.VII

1927 Charles Lindbergh makes the first nonstop solo flight across the Atlantic Ocean, flying 3,610 miles in 33$\frac{1}{2}$ hours

1929 Byrd flies over the South Pole in a Ford Tri-Motor

1929 First U.S. Women's Air Derby

1929 First airship flight around the world by German ship *Graf Zeppelin*

1930

1930 First airline stewardess, Ellen Church, is hired by United Airlines

1930 First U.S. coast-to-coast passenger airline service begins

1931 British inventor Frank Whittle patents the first tubojet engine

1932 Amelia Earhart becomes the first woman to fly solo across the Atlantic Ocean

1933 Wiley Post is the first person to fly solo around the world

1933 First modern airliner, the Boeing 247, is introduced

1935 Albert Stevens and Orvil Anderson of the United States set an

altitude record in their helium balloon, *Explorer II*, reaching 72,395 feet

1936 Douglas DC-3 begins service

1937 The German airship *Hindenburg* explodes and crashes at Lakehurst, New Jersey

1939 German scientist Hans von Ohain builds and flies the first jet aircraft, a Heinkel He 178

1939 Inventor Igor Sikorsky test-pilots his new design, the first practical helicopter, the VS-300

1940

1939–1945 World War II

1941 Japanese bomb U.S. naval base at Pearl Harbor, Hawaii

1942 First military helicopter design by Igor Sikorsky

1942 First successful launch of Germany's V-2 rocket

1944 First jet fighter flies in combat, the German Messerschmitt Me 262

1944 First British jet fighter, the Gloster Meteor, begins service

1944 Attacks of the Japanese kamikazes

1945 Atomic bombs are dropped on Hiroshima and Nagasaki, Japan from a U.S. B-29

1946 The Soviet Union introduces jet fighters, the MiG-9 and Yak-15

1947 Chuck Yeager becomes the first person to fly faster than the speed of sound in the Bell X-1

1947 The *Spruce Goose*, a flying boat and the largest airplane ever built, flies one mile at an altitude of 80 feet

1949 Test flight of the first jet airliner, the British de Havilland Comet

1950

1950–1953 Korean War

1950 Soviet MiG-15s and American F-80 Shooting Stars meet in first combat between jet fighters in Korea

1952 First jetliner, the de Havilland Comet, enters service

1953 American pilot Jacqueline Cochran becomes the first woman to fly faster than sound

1953 The North American F-100 Super Sabre becomes the first operational supersonic jet fighter

1956 Lockheed U-2 plane begins flying missions

1957 Sputnik 1, the first satellite, is launched by the Soviet Union

1959 First round-the-world jet passenger service by Pan American Airways Boeing 707

1960

1960 A U-2 spy plane is shot down over the Soviet Union

1961 Yuri Gagarin of the Soviet Union becomes the first human in space, aboard Vostok 1

1961 Alan Shepard becomes the first American in space, in Mercury *Freedom 7*

1961 U.S. President John F. Kennedy makes a speech announcing that America will place a man on the Moon and return him safely to Earth before 1970

1962 John Glenn is the first American to orbit the Earth, in Mercury *Friendship 7*

1962 The Cuban Missile Crisis

1962 First flight of the Lockheed SR-71 Blackbird reconnaissance plane

1963 Cosmonaut Valentina Tereshkova of the Soviet Union becomes the first woman in space

1964 Gulf of Tonkin resolution passed by Congress, giving President Lyndon Johnson war powers to command attacks in Vietnam

1964 Mariner 4 reaches Mars and transmits images to Earth

1965 Soviet cosmonaut Alexei Leonov takes the first spacewalk

1965 Gemini 4 astronaut Edward White

is the first American to take a spacewalk, lasting 22 minutes

1969 Apollo 11 astronauts Neil Armstrong and Edwin "Buzz" Aldrin become the first humans to land on the Moon

1970

1970 The first jumbo jet, the Boeing 747, enters service

1971 First use of the Apollo Lunar Rover to explore the Moon

1971 The Soviet Union launches the first space station, Salyut 1

1971 First probe to successfully orbit Mars—U.S. Mariner 9

1972 The last two Apollo missions, Apollo 16 and Apollo 17, land on the Moon

1973 First flyby of Jupiter—U.S. probe Pioneer 10

1973 The United States launches the first American space station, Skylab

1974 First flyby of Mercury—U.S. probe Mariner 10

1975 In the Apollo-Soyuz Test Project, the first joint space mission of two nations, an American and Soviet spacecraft dock in space

1976 The first scheduled commercial flights of the Concorde, the first supersonic jetliner

1976 U.S. probes Viking 1 and 2 orbit and land on Mars

1978 U.S. probe Pioneer-Venus 1 orbits Venus

1979 American Bryan Allen pilots the *Gossamer Albatross* in the first human-powered flight across the English Channel

1979 First flyby of Saturn—U.S. probe Pioneer 11

1980

1980 Flyby of Saturn—U.S. probe Voyager 1

1981 Testing begins on stealth fighter,

the Lockheed F-117A

1981 First flight of a U.S. space shuttle, the *Columbia*

1983 Astronaut Sally Ride becomes the first American woman in space on the shuttle *Challenger*

1983 First shuttle mission with Spacelab

1986 Record set for first nonstop non-refueled flight around the world by the Rutan *Voyager*

1986 Space shuttle *Challenger* explodes seconds after launch, killing all crew members

1986 The Soviet Union launches its space station Mir

1986 Flyby of Uranus—U.S. probe Voyager 2

1989 First flight of the B-2 stealth bomber

1989 Flyby of Neptune—U.S. probe Voyager 2

1990

1990 Hubble Space Telescope launched

1990–1991 Persian Gulf War

1991 Lockheed F-117 stealth fighter becomes the first stealth aircraft in combat in the Gulf War

1994 Test flight of the Boeing 777 jetliner, the first aircraft designed completely by computer

1997 U.S. probe Mars Global Surveyor reaches Mars orbit and begins imaging of the planet's surface

1997 U.S. probe Pathfinder lands on Mars and deploys a remote-controlled rover to explore, photograph, and analyze chemicals in rocks

1998 Work begins on building the International Space Station (ISS)

1999 The *Breitling Orbiter 3* makes the first round-the-world balloon trip

2000

2000 An Air France Concorde crashes on takeoff; all Concordes grounded

2000 First crew of Americans and

Russians is placed on the International Space Station

2001 The Russian space station Mir is abandoned and allowed to fall, burning up in the atmosphere

2001 U.S. Mars Odyssey launched to orbit Mars and study the planet

2001 First spacewalk by a Canadian astronaut, Chris Hadfield. He helps install a new robotic arm on the International Space Station

2001 Dennis A. Tito, the first "Space Tourist," pays $20 million for an eight-day trip aboard a Soyuz and the International Space Station

2002 Mars Odyssey spacecraft begins mapping the planet, following a 286 million-mile journey

2003 National Air and Space Museum's new Steven F. Udvar-Hazy Center at Washington Dulles International Airport

2003 Iraqi War begins

2003 Space shuttle *Columbia* disintegrates during re-entry; all seven crew members aboard die

2003 Galaxy Evolution Explorer (GALEX), using an ultraviolet telescope, explores the origins and evolution of galaxies and stars

2005 Space shuttle *Discovery* makes first Return to Flight mission since the loss of *Columbia*

2006 Astronomers rule that Pluto is not a planet

2006 NASA's Mars Orbiter finds signs of "recent water" in Mars gulley

2006 NASA unveils design for Orion spacecraft for carrying crews to orbit the Moon and serve as a Mars crew-return vehicle

Glossary

aeronautics The science of heavier-than-air flight.

ailerons Movable devices on airplane wings used to make the aircraft bank.

airfoil A structure such as a wing or propeller blade that generates lift when moving rapidly through the air.

air lock An airtight chamber that separates areas of different air pressure on a spacecraft.

aerobatics The art of performing precision maneuvers or stunts in the air.

airplane A powered heavier-than-air aircraft.

airship A steerable, lighter-than-air craft powered by an engine.

astronaut A person trained to fly and work aboard a spacecraft.

atmosphere A layer of gases, including oxygen, surrounding the Earth.

autogiro An airplane that has an unpowered rotor that spins freely.

aviation The operation of heavier-than-air aircraft.

balloon A lighter-than-air craft made by filling a large bag with gas lighter than surrounding air.

bank When the pilot raises one wing and lowers the other during a turn.

barnstormers Traveling stunt fliers who performed after World War I.

biplane A fixed-wing airplane with two sets of wings, one on top of the other.

bombsight An instrument that tells bomber crews when to release a bomb to hit a target.

buffeting The shaking of an aircraft as it nears the speed of sound and encounters shock waves.

catapult A powerful device that launches airplanes from aircraft carriers.

cockpit The compartment where the pilot sits to control an airplane or spacecraft.

combustion chamber The part of a rocket where fuel and oxidizer are mixed and ignited to produce hot gases that create thrust.

cosmonaut Russian term for astronaut.

crawler A huge, powerful tracked vehicle used to transport spacecraft to launch pads.

dock When two or more spacecraft join in space.

dogfight An air battle during war between two or more fighter planes.

drag Resistance created by an airplane's shape that hinders its movement through the air.

elevator A movable control on an airplane that makes it climb or descend.

flak Fire from antiaircraft guns.

float plane A seaplane supported on the water by floats.

flying boat A seaplane supported on water by a boatlike hull rather than floats, or pontoons.

flying wing An aircraft with only wing surfaces.

fuselage The body of an airplane.

glider An unpowered, heavier-than-air craft.

gondola The passenger or crew compartment of a balloon or airship.

heavier-than-air Of greater weight than the air that is displaced.

heat shield A barrier of protective material on the outside of a spacecraft to shield it from the intense heat of reentering Earth's atmosphere.

helicopter An aircraft that gets vertical lift from a powered rotor.

jumbo jet A wide-bodied jetliner designed to carry hundreds of passengers.

kamikaze A Japanese suicide pilot who flew bomb-laden planes into Allied warships during World War II.

lighter-than-air Of less weight than the air that is displaced.

kite A tethered glider of paper or cloth stretched over a framework that flies in the wind.

lift The upward force created by air passing around an airfoil.

lifting body Wingless aircraft created to test early space-plane designs.

liftoff The point at which a rocket ignites and launches into the sky.

Mach number A measure of the speed of an aircraft compared to the speed of sound. Mach 1.0 is the speed of sound.

Mission Control The NASA facility that monitors manned spaceflights at Johnson Space Center in Houston, Texas.

mission specialist An astronaut trained to perform a special task or tasks during spaceflight.

monoplane A fixed-wing airplane with one set of wings.

module A section of a spacecraft.

orbit To circle a planet, star, or other body in space.

ornithopter A flying machine with flapping wings, like those of a bird.

oxidizer A substance, such as liquid oxygen, that allows combustion of a fuel in a rocket combustion chamber.

parachute A canopy of fabric attached to rigging and harness, used for emergency exits from aircraft or to drop supplies.

payload The cargo a spacecraft carries.

pitch The motion of an aircraft's nose up or down.

pressure suit A sealed suit designed to maintain normal air pressure around a pilot's body in the lowered atmospheric pressure of high altitudes.

probe An unmanned spacecraft sent to study a body in outer space.

propellant The combined rocket fuel and oxidizer a rocket engine burns to create thrust.

propeller One or more blades rotating on a shaft and driven by an engine to turn and propel an airplane through the air.

radar A system of using radio beams to navigate or locate objects in the air.

reconnaissance plane An aircraft designed to take photographs and spy over enemy territory.

reentry When a spacecraft returns from space and passes through Earth's atmosphere.

rocket A vehicle used to launch spacecraft into space. Also a device or weapon using rocket power.

roll The movement of an aircraft when it rotates, with one wing going up and the other down.

rotor An assembly of rotating wings, called blades, that provide lift for a helicopter or autogiro.

rudder A movable control, usually at the rear of an airplane, that makes the plane turn left or right horizontally.

satellite An object orbiting a larger body in space, such as a weather satellite orbiting Earth.

seaplane An aircraft that can take off and land on water.

sound barrier An invisible barrier of extreme turbulence and drag an aircraft encounters when it reaches the speed of sound.

space The region beyond Earth's atmosphere.

space shuttle A reusable craft used to travel into space.

stall When an aircraft moves so slowly its wings cannot produce lift and it falls.

stealth aircraft Aircraft capable of flying into enemy territory without being detected.

streamlined With a smooth shape to reduce air resistance, or drag.

supersonic Flying faster than the speed of sound.

thermal A rising body of warm air used by birds and gliders to gain height.

thrust The pushing force created by a propeller or by a jet or rocket engine that propels an aircraft or spacecraft.

triplane An airplane with three sets of wings, one on top of another.

weightlessness The absence of notable effects of gravity.

wing warping A system that uses control wires to twist, or warp, the wings to achieve control over roll during flight.

yaw The movement of an airplane's nose from side to side.

zero gravity Also called zero G, this is the state of apparent weightlessness that astronauts feel when floating in space.

zeppelin A rigid lighter-than-air airship of the kind first created by Count Ferdinand von Zeppelin of Germany during World War I.

Index

Picture Credits

Position on page: B= bottom, T= top, C= center, L= left, R= right

Sources: NASM = Smithsonian National Air and Space Museum, SI = Smithsonian Institution, NASA = National Aeronautics and Space Administration, NASA-ARC = NASA Ames Research Center, NASA-KSC = NASA Kennedy Space Center, NASA-JSC = NASA Johnson Space Center, NASA-DRFC = NASA Dryden Flight Research Center, NASA-MSFC = NASA Marshall Space Flight Center, NASA-LARC = NASA Langley Aeronautical Research Center, NASA-SSC = NASA Stennis Space Center, USAF = U. S. Air Force, DOD = Department of Defense.

Front Cover: NASA-KSC KSC-92PC-1895; **1:** NASM-1A10506; **2-3:** © 2000 USAF Thunderbirds, photo by TSgt Kevin Gruenwald; **5:** NASA-JSC SL3-115-1837; **8 TR, 9:** Carolyn Russo, NASM; **10-11:** Interface Multimedia, © 1999 SI; **10 B:** Eric F. Long, NASM; **12 BL:** SI-A-3379-M; **12 TC:** NASM (TMS-A19640490000); **12-13:** SI-93-2342; **13 T:** SI-A-627-B; **13 CL:** SI-A-30908-A; **13 CR:** SI-A-39013; **13 BL:** NASM Poster Collection (SI 98-20121); **13 BR:** SI-A-31421; **14 C:** SI-87-17019; **14 B:** SI 4x5 A&I Coll. 12583; **14-15 C:** © 1933 SI, Garnet Jex, *Langley Model #5 and Houseboat* (SI 96-15732); **14-15 B:** Eric F. Long, NASM (SI 94-2198); **15 TR:** NASM-1A32841; **15 TCR:** NASM-1A15248; **15 BCR:** NASM-9A00001; **16 CL:** © Carl R. Sams II; **16 B**: Mark Avino, NASM (SI 97-15333)**; 16-17 C:** SI-A-26767-B; **16-17 B:** SI-A-42363; **17 TR:** © 2001 Howard S. Friedman; **17 CR:** SI-A-41898-E; **17 BR:** Eric F. Long, NASM (TMS-A19640054000), SI; **18 BL:** SI-A-38681-B; **18-19:** SI-86-9865; **19 TL:** SI-A-42783-L; **19 TR:** SI-85-10844; **20 CL:** Georges Naudet Collection, NASM (SI 85-17170); **20 BR:** SI-87-10389; **20 TR:** SI-96-16073; **20-21:** Eric F. Long, NASM (SI 94-2184); **21 TL:** SI-72-10099; **21 TR:** SI-89-21352; **21 C:** SI-98-15036; **21 BR:** SI-A-47154; **22 BL:** USAF, courtesy NASM (SI A-3853); **22-23:** J. B. Deneen, *Von Richthofen's Last Flight,* 1971, NASM (SI 86-5656); **22 BR:** NASM-9A00006; **23 BL:** SI-76-13317; **23 TR:** SI-87-16023; **23 CR:** World War I Photographs Collection [Driggs] (1993-0040-TEMP-0001), NASM; **23 BR:** © 1985 United Features Syndicate, Inc.; **24 T:** Robert Soubiran Collection, NASM (SI A-48746-U); **24 BL:** © 2001 Howard S. Friedman; **24-25:** Illustration © John Batchelor; **25 TR:** Mark Avino, NASM (SI 86-12094); **26 CR:** USAF (USAF-29589AC), courtesy NASM; **26-27:** Eric F. Long, NASM (SI 94-2230); **27 TL:** NASM-7A44911; **27 TR:** NASM-7A44903-1; **27 CR:** NASM-7A44903-2; **27 BR:** World War I Exhibit Collection (1993-0063-TEMP-0002), NASM; **28 L:** SI-93-16054; **28 TR:** SI-85-12324-D; **28 BR:** Dale Hrabak, NASM (SI 81-14836); **28-29:** SI-A-4463; **29 TL:** SI-85-12346-A; **29 TR:** NASM Poster Collection (SI 98-20079); **29 CR:** SI-89-1182; **29 BL:** SI-87-10374; **29 BR:** SI-94-4476; **30 BL:** SI-77-11793; **30 BR:** Carolyn Russo, NASM (SI Neg 93-5512); **30-31:** © 1982 Ralph B. Steele, *The* Winnie Mae *at the Volga, 1931*, courtesy NASM; **31 TC:** NASM Poster Collection (SI 98-20101); **31 TR:** NASM-2A40088; **31 CR:** NASM-2A40311; **31 BR:** SI-A-43352; **32 TL:** Eric F. Long, NASM (SI 99-40459); **32 B:** SI-A-32568-B; **32-33 T:** Eric F. Long, NASM (SI 2001-1890); **32-33 B:** Eric F. Long, NASM (SI 94-2285); **33 TR:** SI-75-2186; **34 BL:** SI-76-2177; **34-35 T:** SI-76-17446; **34-35 B:** USAF, courtesy NASM (SI 83-8854); **35 TC:** Mark Avino, NASM (SI 97-15335); **35 TR:** SI-76-15516; **35 C:** © 2001 Howard S. Friedman; **35 BR:** NASM-1A46344; **36 BL:** SI-A-336; **36-37:** Eric F. Long, NASM; **37 T:** Dane Penland, NASM (SI 79-763); **37 C:** Eric F. Long, NASM; **37 BC:** SI-A-42065-A; **37 BR:** SI-78-17771; **38 BL:** SI-86-10744; **38-39 T:** SI-73-4032; **38-39 C:** SI-A-45874; **39 BR:** Dane Penland, NASM (SI 80-2082); **38-39 B:** NASM-2B07750; **41 BL:** SI-78-13936; **40 TR:** Nathaniel L. Dewell Collection, NASM (SI 89-7061); **40 CR:** Dane Penland, NASM (SI 80-2101); **41 TL:** Boeing Historical Archives, (SI 80-12338); **41 TR:** SI-91-14177; **41 C:** SI-A-42344-E; **40 CL:** SI-90-10186; **40 C:** Airline Baggage Label Collection, NASM (SI 93-15843); **40 BL:** SI-90-10182; **42 CL:** Delta Air Lines, courtesy NASM (TMS-A19950279000), SI; **42 CT:** NASM (TMS-A19711461000), SI; **42 CB:** NASM (TMS-A19710687022), SI; **42 BL:** SI-A-1932; **42-43:** American Airlines, Inc. (NASM-7A21713); **43 TC:** SI-97-15046; **43 TR:** SI-89-1216; **43 CT:** NASM Poster Collection (SI 98-20756); **43 C:** American Airlines, Inc. (NASM Poster Collection, SI 98-20292); **43 CR:** Airline Baggage Label Collection, NASM; **43 BC:** NASM Poster Collection (SI 98-20518); **43 BR:** NASM Airline Baggage Label Collection; **44 BL:** SI-85-19411; **44 TR:** NASM Poster Collection (SI 98-20504); **44 CR:** SI-94-1938; **44 BR:** SI-A-945-A; **44-45:** USAF, courtesy NASM (SI 98-15068); **46 TR:** SI-80-9016; **46-47:** Eric F. Long, NASM (SI 94-2306); **44 BR:** SI-89-9947; **47 TL:** SI-96-16068; **47 C:** SI-80-17077; **48 BL:** SI-2000-9714; **48 TC:** USAF, courtesy NASM (SI 97-17491); **48 BR:** USAF, courtesy NASM (SI 97-17480); **48-49 T:** Eric F. Long, NASM (SI 97-15875); **48-49 C:** USAF, courtesy NASM (SI 98-15407); **49 TR:** Dane Penland, NASM (SI 80-2093); **49 CR:** SI-81-896; **49 BR:** Richard B. Farrar, NASM (SI 74-4295); **50 BL:** SI-85-7272; **50 TR:** NASM Poster Collection (SI 98-20672); **50-51:** © 1978 Frank Wootton, *Achtung, Spitfire!*; **51 TR:** NASM Poster Collection (SI 98-20001); **52 BL:** USAF, courtesy NASM (SI A-46594-F); **52-53:** USAF, courtesy NASM (SI 98-15545); **53 TR:** Eric F. Long, NASM (SI 97-15363); **53 CR:** Ross Chapple, NASM (SI-2001-1899); **53 BL:** USAF, courtesy NASM (SI 2001-2047); **53 BR:** USAF photo, courtesy NASM (SI 91-1471); **54 BL:** SI-99-42462; **54-55:** R. G. Smith, *Douglas SBD-3*, © NASM, gift of the MPB Corporation (SI 95-8196); **55 TR:** Eric F. Long, NASM (SI 2000-9387); **55 BR:** U.S. Navy, courtesy NASM (SI 85-7306); **56 BL:** NASM Poster Collection (SI 98-20692); **56-57:** Eric Long and Mark Avino, NASM (SI 98-15873); **57 TR:** USAF, courtesy NASM (SI 2001-1900); **57 BR:** USAF, courtesy NASM (SI 2000-4554); **58 BL:** USAF, courtesy NASM (SI 86-4483); **58 TR:** Eric F. Long, NASM; **58-59:** USAF, courtesy NASM (SI 97-17485); **59 TR:** © 2001 Howard S. Friedman; **58-59 BL:** Illustration © John Batchelor; **59 CR:** SI-75-16331-B; **59 BR:** Dale Hrabak, NASM (SI-79-4623); **60 TL:** Richard Rash, NASM (SI 2001-1889); **60 CL:** SI-80-5653; **60 CR:** USAF, courtesy NASM (NASM-7A33647), SI; **60 BL:** NASM-7A33601; **60 BR:** SI-97-16672; **60-61:** Frank Wootton, *Night Reconnaissance Over Vietnam,* 1978, NASM, SI; **61 TR:** Richard Keller, NASM (SI 2001-1887); **61 CR:** NASM-1B37661; **61 BR:** Courtesy of Fairchild, via NASM (NASM-1B33031), SI; **62 BL:** USAF; **62 TL:** USAF photo by Staff Sgt. Douglas C. Brunelle; **62-63:** US Navy photo by Chief Petty Officer Troy D. Summers; **63 TR:** NASA-AC85-0740-13; **63 CR:** DOD; **63 BR:** US Navy photo by Petty Officer 3rd Class Nick Magdaleno; **64 BL:** USAF photo by Staff Sgt. Gary R. Coppage; **64 TR:** USAF photo by Tech Sgt. James D. Mossman; **64 CR:** USAF photo by Staff Sgt. Steve Thurow; **64 BR:** NASA-DRFC-EC95-43249-04; **64-65 T:** USAF photo by by Staff Sgt. Andy Dunaway; **65 BL, BR:** © 2000 USAF Thunderbirds, photo by TSgt Kevin Gruenwald; **66 CL:** USAF photo by by Master Sgt. Rose Reynolds; **66 BL:** Eric F. Long, NASM SI (SI 99-15007); **66 TR:** NASM 9A-00030; **66-67:** SI-98-41062; **67 TR:** NASA-DRFC EC94-42883-4; **67 CR, BR:** USAF; **68 BL:** NASA-ARC; **68 TR:** Boeing Historical Archives (SI-88-14302); **68-69:** USAF; **69 BL:** NASM-1A14822; **69 TR:** © British Aerospace, photo by Adrian Meredith; **69 BR:** Eric F. Long, NASM (SI 2001-1903); **70 BL:** SI-92-706; **70-71:** Eric F. Long, NASM (SI 2000-9362); **71 BL:** SI 2001-1888; **71 TR:** NASM-1B10487; **71 CTR:** NASM-9A00009; **71 CBR:** © 1999 Ed Kashi; **71 BR:** U. S. Coast Guard; **72 BR:** Eric F. Long and Mark Avino, NASM (SI 2001-1877); **72 TR. BR:** National Oceanic and Atmospheric Administration / Department of Commerce, Flying with NOAA Collection (fly00269 and fly00017); **73 TL:** Hans Groenhoff Photographic Collection, NASM (SI 2001-1902); **73 CL:** Boeing Historical Archives; **73 TR:** DoD photo by Tech. Sgt. Lono Kollars, USAF; **73 CR:** USAF photo by Scott Spitzer; **73 BR:** DoD photo by Staff Sgt. Jerry Morrison, USAF; **74 BL:** © Budd Davisson (SI-2001-1891); **74-75:** © James A. Sugar; **75 TL:** NASA-DFRC ECN-12604; **75 TR:** © Breitling SA, courtesy NASM (NASM 9A-00020); **75 CR:** Carolyn Russo, NASM; **75 BR:** © Breitling SA, courtesy NASM (NASM 9A-00017); **76 L:** SI-A-5367; **76 BC:** SI-77-14261; **76 R:** © 2001 Howard S. Friedman; **76-77:** SI-77-1020; **77 BL:** SI-73-7925; **77 T:** B. Anthony Stewart, © 1940 National Geographic Society; **77 CL:** © Clark University (SI-A-44528-A); **77 CR:** © Clark University (SI-A-42103); **78 BL:** Eric F. Long, NASM (TMS-A19751576000), SI; **78 TR:** NASM (TMS-A19711115000), SI; **78 CTR:** NASA-DRFC EC88-0180-4; **78 BR:** NASA-DRFC ECN-225; **78-79:** Eric F. Long, NASM (SI 94-2284); **79 BL:** NASA-DRFC EC65-884; **79 BR:** NASA-DRFC EC61-0034; **80 BL:** NASA-LARC EL-1996-00089; **80 TR:** NASA 61-MR3-109; **80-81 T:** NASA-JSC S65-30428; **80-81 B:** NASA-JSC S64-22331; **81 TR:** NASA-JSC S65-63197; **81 CTR:** Eric F. Long, NASM (SI 97-16235); **81 CBR:** NASA-JSC S62-00303; **81 BR:** Eric F. Long, NASM (SI 98-15802-11); **82 L:** NASA-JSC S69-39961; **82 BC:** NASA M-108; **82-83 T:** NASA-KSC KSC-69P-0168; **82-83 B:** all rocket drawings © Peter Alway; **83 TR:** NASA-KSC KSC-92PC-1895; **84 BL:** Eric F. Long, NASM (SI 99-15165-6); **84 TC:** Eric F. Long, NASM (SI 99-15195); **84-85 T:** Fred Freeman, *Saturn Blockhouse,* 1968, NASM; **84-85 B:** Eric F. Long, NASM (SI 99-15164-2); **85 R:** NASA; **86 BL:** NASA-JSC S69-38749; **86-87:** NASA-JSC AS11-40-5868; **87 TR:** NASA-JSC S69-31740; **87 CR:** NASA-JSC S75-29715; **87 BR:** NASA 69-H-1421; **88 BL:** Mark Avino, NASM (SI 97-15094); **88-89:** Eric F. Long, NASM (SI 2000-9371); **89 TR:** NASA-JSC S71-21244; **89 BR:** NASA-JSC AS12-49-7278; **90 L:** Eric F. Long, NASM (SI 98-15805); **90 BC:** NASA-JSC AS16-117-18825; **90 B:** NASA AS16-107-17432 through AS16-107-17440; **90-91:** NASA-JSC AS16-114-18423; **92 BL:** NASA-JSC AS16-117-18840; NASA-JSC AS16-117-18841; **92 TR:** NASA-JSC AS12-51-7510; **92 CR:** NASA-JSC AS16-113-18294; **92-93:** NASA-KSC AS11 44-6642; **94 BL:** NASA-JSC S72-15409; **94 TC:** NASA-JSC S73-23952; **94-95:** NASA-JSC SL14-143-4706; **95 TL:** NASA-JSC SL3-108-1307; **95 TR:** NASA-JSC SL3-108-1278; **95 TR:** © 2001 Howard S. Friedman; **95 C:** NASA-JSC S73-24315; **95 CTR:** NASA-JSC SL3-108-1292; **95 CBR:** NASA-JSC S73-38687; **96 CTL:** NASM (TMS-A19740481000); **96 CBL:** courtesy The Perot Foundation; **96 BL:** Lent by the Museum of the Yuri Gagarin Cosmonauts Training Center, Star City, Russia; **96 TR:** NASA-JSC S75-33375; **96 BR:** SI-75-10226; **96-97:** Andrei Sokolov, *Soyuz-Apollo Over the Caspian Sea*, 1975, NASM; **97 TR:** NASA-JSC S75-20361; **97 CTR:** NASA-JSC S75-29432; **97 CBR:** NASA-JSC AST-03-175; **97 BR:** Eric F. Long, NASM (SI 97-16108); **98 TL:** Eric F. Long, NASM (SI 98-15012); **98 TR:** Eric F. Long, NASM (SI 98-15587); **98 BL:** Wright/McCook Field Still Photograph Collection (WF-42364), NASM; **98 BC:** Courtesy of Fairchild, NASM (SI 88-32); **98 BR:** NASA, courtesy of NASM (SI 2001-1901); **98-99:** NASA; **99 TR:** NASA-KSC KSC-00PP-0532; **100 BL:** NASA-KSC KSC-99PP-1337; **100 R:** NASA-KSC KSC-99PP-0532; **100-101:** NASA-SSC 96-PC-828; **102 BL:** NASA-JSC STS068-67-013; **102 BC:** NASA-JSC S88-26662; **102-103**: Eric F. Long, NASM (SI 2000-9349); **103:** NASA-KSC KSC-96PC-1041; **104 BL:** NASA S99-E-5065; **104-105:** Eric F. Long and Mark Avino, NASM (SI 2001-2277); **106-107:** Illustration © John Batchelor; **108 L:** NASA-MSFC 9263351; **108-109:** NASA-JSC STS061-48-001; **109 TR:** NASA, The Hubble Heritage Team (STScI/AURA, STScI-PRC00-12); **109 BR:** NASA and Hubble Heritage Team (STScI-PRC99-41); **110 CL:** NASA-KSC; **110 BL:** © 1989 Glavkosmos, courtesy NASM Poster Collection; **110-111:** NASA-JSC STS071-S-072; **111 TR:** © 2001 Howard S. Friedman; **111 BR:** NASA-JSC STS76-713036; **112 TL:** NASA-JSC ; **112 TR:** Eric F. Long, NASM (SI 98-15574-43); **112-113 C:** Eric F. Long, NASM (SI 2000-3882); **112-113 B:** NASA-KSC; **113 TR:** NASA-JSC STS051-10-025; **113 CL:** NASA MSFC 9500974; **113 CR:** NASA-JSC STS007-26-1438; **114-115:** NASA-KSC KSC-96PC-1334; **115 T:** NASA-KSC KSC-92PC-1461; **115 C:** NASA-DRFC EC91-659-2; **115 B:** NASA-DRFC EC98-44740-2; **116-117:** NASA MSFC 9802675; **118 BL:** NASA-DRFC EC00-0096-77; **118 BC:** NASA STS101-714-028; **118 TR:** NASA STS101-716-079; **118-119:** NASA MSFC 9503938; **120 BL:** NASA-DRFC ED98-44824-1; **120 TR:** © 2001 Patrick Kam; **120-121:** NASA-DRFC ED98-44831; **121 TR:** NASA-DRFC ED97-43968-4; **121 TCR:** NASA-LARC EL-1997-00038; **121 BCR:** NASA-LARC EL1997-00059; **121 BR:** NASA MSFC-00789/9905003; **122-123:** All art by Pat Rawlings, courtesy NASA; **123 B:** Map by US Geological Survey, courtesy NASM Center for Earth and Planetary Studies (CEPS).

Source Notes

Quotes used in this book have been taken from the following sources:

p. 17: A letter from Orville Wright to a friend.

p. 23: Manfred von Richthofen, from an autobiographical account, *The Red Baron*, as quoted in *Aviation History* by Anne Millbrooke (Englewood, Colorado: Jeppesen Sanderson, Inc., 1999).

p. 25: Dominick A. Pisano, et al, *Memory and the Great War in the Air* (Seattle: University of Washington Press for the Smithsonian Institution, 1992).

p. 36: Charles A. Lindbergh, *The Spirit of St. Louis* (New York: Charles Scribners Sons, 1953).

p. 39: Amelia Earhart, *Last Flight* (New York: Harcourt Brace and Company, 1937).

p. 48: A letter of U.S. combat fighter pilot Quentin C. Aanenson to his fiancee, Jackie, in 1944.

p. 51: A speech to Parliament by British Prime Minister Winston Churchill, August 1940.

p. 58: Chuck Yeager, *Yeager* (New York: Bantam Books, 1985).

p. 75: Bertrand Piccard and Brian Jones, *Around the World in 20 Days: The Story of Our History-Making Balloon Flight* (New York: John Wiley & Sons, Inc., 1999).

p. 86: Neil Armstrong in a televised landing on the Moon, July 20, 1969.

p. 100: John Young, upon landing after the first space shuttle flight aboard the shuttle *Columbia,* April 12, 1981.

p. 101: Robert L. Crippen in comments on the same landing.

p. 113: Sally Ride with Susan Okie, *To Space & Back* (New York: Lothrop, Lee and Shepard Books, 1986).

For Further Reading

Berliner, Don. *Distance Flights*. Minneapolis: Lerner, 1990.

Blackburn, Ken and Jeff Lammers. *The World Record Paper Airplane Book*. New York: Workman, 1994.

Briggs, Carole. *At the Controls: Women in Aviation*. Minneapolis: Lerner, 1991.

Collins, Martin. *After Sputnik: 50 Years of the Space Age*. New York: HarperCollins, 2007.

Craddock, Robert. *Apollo 11 Box: Artifacts from the First Lunar Landing*. San Francisco: Chronicle Books, 2003.

Doherty, Paul, Dan Rathjen and Exploratorium Teacher Institute Staff. *The Spinning Blackboard and Other Dynamic Experiments on Force and Motion*. New York: John Wiley & Sons, 1996.

Furniss, Tim, David J. Shayler, and Michael D. Shayler. *Praxis Manned Spaceflight Log* New York: Springer-Praxis, 2007.

Grant, R.G. *Flight: 100 Years of Aviation*. London: DK Publishing, 2002.

Hardesty, Von. *Great Aviators and Epic Flights*. Westport, Conn.: Hugh Lauter Levin, 2003.

Jakab, Peter L. and Tom Crouch. *The Wright Brothers and the Invention of the Aerial Age*. Washington, D.C.: National Geographic, 2003.

Jennings, Terry J. *Planes, Gliders, Helicopters, and Other Flying Machines*. New York: Larousse Kingfisher Books, 1995.

Long, Eric, Mark Avino, Dana Bell. *In the Cockpit: Inside 50 History-Making Aircraft*. New York: HarperCollins, 2007.

Long, Eric, Mark Avino, Tom Alison, Dana Bell. *At the Controls: The National Air and Space Museum Book of Cockpits*. Erin, Ont.: Boston Mills Press, 2001.

van der Linden, F. Robert, ed. *Best of the National Air and Space Museum*. New York: HarperCollins, 2006.

Winchester, Jim. *Space Missions from Sputnik to SpaceShipOne*. San Diego, Calif.: Thunder Bay Press, 2006.